Our Lord Jesus Christ said eternal life is to know the Father and Jesus Christ whom He has sent (John 17:3). Therefore, there is no enterprise more important than seeking to "know" God. In this splendid and inspired book, Bill Thrasher offers us the core of what he has learned about knowing our heavenly Father through a loving relationship with Jesus Christ.

> — **LYLE W. DORSETT**
> Billy Graham Professor of Evangeli
> Beeson Divinity School, Samford U

The cumulative impact of an orderly survey
in *God As He Wants You to Know Him*, is powe

> — **J. I. PACKER**
> Professor of theology, author of *Knowing God*

Amazingly, this book delivers on its title! This book is having a profound impact on my confidence in and reverence for God. I hope that every seminary, church, small group, and individual will read, study, and discuss this classic.

> — **WAYNE HOPKINS**
> Dean and professor, emeritus, Moody Graduate School of Chicago

I'm convinced the best theologians are not in the ivory tower or the book-lined study. They wear out their shoes down in the trenches with people like you and me. In this book, Dr. William Thrasher gets down on my level and helps me understand the love and mercy and grace of God. This is one of the most important topics you'll ever study by a man who walks with God and has a heart for His people.

> — **CHRIS FABRY**
> Radio host and author

For thirty years I have been pursuing the core of the core of God's global mission that led to the 10/40 Window geographic focus and the 4/14 Window demographic focus. Bill Thrasher's book *God As He Wants You to Know Him* gets to the core of how to develop a personal relationship with God and make a difference in this world. Transform the individual and you will transform the world.

> — **LUIS BUSH**
> International Facilitator, Transform World Connections

The book is thorough, rich with Scripture that describes the attributes of God, and very practical. The truth of knowing God becomes a great source of personal encouragement to the reader.

> — **DAVE CORTNER**
> Pastor, Bethel Baptist Church, Cherry Hill, New Jersey

God As He Wants You to Know Him exudes the same combination of careful scholarship and devotional warmth that make Dr. Thrasher's classes well worth attending. This book would be a wonderful foundation for discipleship, teaching, or pastoral training.

> — **PETER GRANT**
> Founder and President, PreVision Partnership

The strength and usefulness of this important work is found in how Bill Thrasher personalizes the study of God's attributes.
— **RICHARD YOOK**
    Physician, member of Board of Trustees
    Moody Bible Institute

Bill Thrasher's thorough writings offer the gateway to a rich life in Christ by biblically developing the attributes of God in a profound yet practical manner. It will be impossible to read this stimulating work without a highlighter and a pen.
— **DAVID R. PENDLEY**
    President, Avenue Mortgage Corporation

This book encouraged me greatly in my own thinking about our glorious God, and I already have recommended it to several people in our church!
— **STEVE FARISH**
    Senior Pastor, Crossroads Church, Grayslake, Illinois

Rarely have I read a more practical, accessible, tenderly instructive presentation of the attributes of God. This book captures in one volume the exemplary application of biblical and theological truth with which all Bill's students are richly acquainted.
— **L. DARYLE WORLEY JR.**
    Pastor/Teacher, Grace Church of DuPage, Illinois

If you want to know what God is like and how to have an intimate relationship with Him, read this book. I think it is a must-read for anyone who would like a clearer understanding of the character and nature of God. It could change your life. It has mine.
— **PAUL H. JOHNSON**
    Former Board of Trustees chairman, Moody Bible Institute

Knowing God as he has revealed himself is essential for a satisfying spiritual life. Dr. Bill Thrasher writes from a deep personal relationship with the God who has revealed himself.
— **JOHN A. JELINEK**
    Vice President, academic dean, and professor
    Moody Theological Seminary

Bill Thrasher has been a dear friend and colleague for many years. This book flows from the model of his life! Bill truly is a "man of one thing," committed to knowing God and spending his life that others may know Him as well.
— **JOHN FUDER**
    Director, Justice & Compassion Ministries
    Resource Global/Heart For The City

In a day when so many Christian books are based on feeling and experience, it is encouraging to read a volume that is biblically sub-

stantive. I wholeheartedly commend it to the family of God.
> — **DON CURRIN**
> HeartCry Missionary Society, Eastern Europe Coordinator

Here is a book that always points you back to the Good Book. Scripture citations abound on every page. But don't stop there! Thrasher doesn't just want you to know the Bible — he wants you to know the God about whom the Bible speaks!
> — **BRYAN LITFIN**
> Professor of theology, Moody Bible Institute

This book encouraged me to delight in God throughout my day, every day of my life. God is a God of relationship, and Dr. Bill Thrasher shows us how to focus on God's attributes as He displays those attributes in and through our lives.
> — **DOREEN GAGLIANO**
> Health policy analyst, centers for Medicare
> and Medicaid services

Reading this work on the perfections of God is a profound lesson in theology and a moving devotional experience at the same time. It is written by a mature scholar who models its principles in daily life.
> — **DAN GREEN**
> Professor, Moody Theological Seminary

This book will move the reader into a place of deeper intimacy with God and is a must for any discipleship relationship. I plan on using it with those God sends me to mentor.
> — **GEORGE MOSHER**
> Registrar, Moody Bible Institute

We all wonder, What is God like? In this book Dr. Bill Thrasher gives us the answer — with the intent that our lives would be changed and conformed to the likeness of God's Son.
> — **GREG BARR**
> Missionary to Quebec, CrossWorld

A must-read for every believer! There is no better answer to every challenge or problem we face than to understand and know God. This book will renew and refresh your relationship with the God you can know.
> — **KEVIN HOWELLS**
> Pastor of Small Groups, Park Community Church, Chicago

In a culture that seeks to know God on its own terms, Bill Thrasher's book provides a biblically based, practical path forward for those who want to know God as He desires to be known.
> — **J. BRIAN TUCKER**
> Associate professor of New Testament
> Moody Theological Seminary

In this book you will encounter the character of God and the practical ramifications His character should have on you every day. If you live out these truths, your life will be forever transformed.

> — **MATT SHADA**
> Lead Pastor, Steadfast Bible Fellowship, Omaha, Nebraska

What makes this book so inviting is the author's personal application of its truths in his own life and his longing for his readers to do the same. Doctrine truly is devotional!

> — **CECIL SANDERS**
> Senior Pastor, First Baptist Church, Headland, Alabama

I am always looking for resources to help people grow in their walk with the Lord, especially those who are new believers in Christ. I can't think of anything more important than understanding the character of God as we seek to conform more and more to His image.

> — **JEREMIAH CLAPPER**
> Pastor, Living Rock Church in Gillette, Wyoming

Soundly doctrinal yet practical. One of the best books on the character of God I have ever read. Dr. Thrasher's passionate pursuit of intimacy with Christ has once again led me to a deeper knowledge and experience of knowing God.

> — **JEFF CHUDY**
> Director of Great Lakes Bridges International
> Bloomington, Indiana

The challenge set forth by *God As He Wants You to Know Him* is one I will never forget: Ask God how you may be treating Him impersonally. A must-read for those who desire a more intimate relationship with their heavenly Father.

> — **SCOTT NESSE**
> Pastor, Stone Ridge Church, Rockford, Illinois

Once you begin reading this book you won't want to stop or turn back. It outlines the attributes of God in a way that makes them very personal and inspiring.

> — **ROOSEVELT GIBSON**
> Recording artist, and associate pastor
> Salem Baptist Church, Chicago

What a delight to investigate the character of our amazing God, and to reap the benefits and joy of knowing our Creator and the One with whom we'll spend eternity.

> — **ROGER BURGESS**
> Associate principal, Wheaton Christian Grammar School

God
As He Wants You to Know Him

BILL THRASHER

MOODY PUBLISHERS
CHICAGO

All Scripture quotations are taken from the *New American Standard Bible*®, Copyright © 1960, 1962, 1963, 1968, 1971, 1972, 1973, 1975, 1977, 1995 by The Lockman Foundation. Used by permission. (www.Lockman.org)

Scripture quotations marked KJV are taken from the King James Version.

Edited by Jim Vincent
Interior design: Ragont Design
Cover design: Faceout Studio
Cover image: Magone / Shutterstock.com

Library of Congress Cataloging-in-Publication Data

Thrasher, Bill, 1952-
    God as he wants you to know him / by Bill Thrasher.
      p. cm.
    Includes bibliographical references.
    ISBN 978-0-8024-0422-0
    1. God (Christianity) — Attributes. I. Title.
  BT130.T59 2012
  231'.4 — dc23
                                        2011051545

We hope you enjoy this book from Moody Publishers. Our goal is to provide high-quality, thought-provoking books and products that connect truth to your real needs and challenges. For more information on other books and products written and produced from a biblical perspective, go to www.moodypublishers or write to:

Moody Publishers
820 N. LaSalle Boulevard
Chicago, IL 60610

3 5 7 9 10 8 6 4 2

Printed in the United States of America

Dedicated to the Lord Jesus Christ, who is the very "image of the invisible God" (Colossians 1:15) and who is the "radiance of His glory" and the "exact representation of His nature" (Hebrews 1:3).

The Lord's kind work in uprooting lies from my mind about His glorious character and replacing them with truth in order to understand the beauty of His person is a gift for which I can never thank Him enough.

Contents

Part Four: A Perfectly Holy, Righteous, Faithful, and Loving Person

Part Five: A Gracious, Merciful, and Good God Who Is Always in Control

Part Six: A Glorious God

Acknowledgments

$\mathcal{I}$ WOULD LIKE TO acknowledge the great aid I have received from my former and present students, who have not only so attentively and enthusiastically listened to my lectures on the character of God but also taught me many truths. In the early part of this project, I happened to meet a former student who had come to celebrate his twenty-fifth graduation anniversary. As I told him of my vision for this book, he responded by telling me how he had reviewed his lecture notes from my class on the attributes of God for the previous twenty-five years. I took Tim's words as God's kind encouragement to begin writing this book.

Words could not adequately express my gratitude to the thousands of other students as well who have been an enormous encouragement to my life since I began teaching in

1980. Scott Wolfe, a current student, has been a valuable help beyond words in typing this manuscript.

I would also like to acknowledge the kind prayers and support of God's people who regularly pray for my life, family, and ministry. Many of them receive prayer updates on a regular basis and so graciously respond in intercession. Once again, at the very beginning of this project, God gave a very special providential meeting one Sunday morning. As I was entering church, I was met by my former seminary classmate Luis Bush who was visiting that day. He asked me how he could pray for me, and I told him about God's prompting to begin this book. He and his dear wife at that very moment put their hands on my back, bowed their heads, and prayed over me. What a special support that was to me from these dear ones who have been so mightily used to encourage missions around the world.

I am also grateful to my wife, Penny, who is a true gift of God, and to my three sons as well as my mother and mother-in-law. All of these are a constant, prayerful encouragement to me and none of my successes could have come without their loving help.

The Moody Publishers team, headed by Greg Thornton, with help on this book by Barnabas Piper and Adam Kellogg, have been a total delight to work with. They live lives that are a great tribute to their Lord. I am greatly indebted as well to the work of senior editor Jim Vincent, who has been extremely helpful in shaping the manuscript to its final form.

I would also like to acknowledge John Jelinek, the current dean of Moody Theological Seminary, as well as my former deans B. Wayne Hopkins and Joe Henriques. Together with my former deans at the Moody Bible Institute (MBI) undergraduate school, Bob Woodburn and Howard Whaley, these men have granted me during the past thirty years the privilege of teaching various college and seminary courses on the spiritual life.

I thank God for the opportunity to have served under the leadership of four presidents at MBI: George Sweeting, Joseph Stowell, Michael Easley, and Paul Nyquist. All have been a gift of God to lead this great institution. My colleagues, whom I have the privilege of laboring with at Moody, as well as the administrative team, have made Moody Bible Institute a very pleasant place to serve our Lord.

Preface

$\mathcal{I}$N MY DOCTORAL STUDIES I read a book by a Scottish theologian, John Dick, entitled *Lectures in Theology*. In this older work, he gave detailed and practical lectures on the attributes of God. I then read the classic *The Existence and Attributes of God*, by Puritan preacher and writer Stephen Charnock. In all of my previous studies in systematic theology, I had not heard practical lectures on the character of God that gave direction, meaning, and purpose for living.

During that time my most heartfelt prayer request became, "Lord, help me aim my life at the right thing." I feared aiming my life at the wrong thing and achieving my aim but later realizing that my ladder was propped up against the wrong wall. I believe that one of the answers to this yearlong prayer request was a newfound emphasis on the character of God. I wrote my doctoral dissertation for my ThD in systematic theology on "The Attributes of God in Pauline Theology."

When I started teaching at Moody Bible Institute in 1980, I was assigned the course that dealt with theology proper. I developed my own lectures on the attributes of God, which I have refined for the past three decades. When curriculum change brought a new course to our school entitled Christian Life and Ethics, I was one of the professors asked to teach this new course. Seeing the enormous help that the emphasis on the character of God had been to me and to many students, I decided to devote a section of the course to this topic. As I developed this course for the first time, I realized that the emphasis should not be merely a section but the very foundation of the course, for it is the very foundation of the Christian life.

Many years ago A. W. Tozer said, "What comes into your mind when you think of God is the most important thing about your life." In his book *You and Your Thoughts*, Earl Radmacher wrote, "Right living begins with right thinking, and right thinking begins with right thinking about God."[1] I believe on the authority of 2 Corinthians 3:18 that a correct focus on the glory of God is the means that the Spirit of God works through to change a believer's life. That is why throughout my teaching of the Christian life for the past thirty-plus years I have declared that the foundation of the spiritual life is right thinking about God.

God As He Wants You to Know Him refers to previous writings I have done in order to help the reader who wishes to look further into specific topics. More importantly, this book will constantly refer to Scripture, because in the final analysis this is the only infallible source. We are totally dependent upon God's revelation of Himself in His Word to know the truth about Him (see Isaiah 55:5; Matthew 11:27; 1 Corinthians 2:11–12; 1 Timothy 6:15–16).

Looking at the character of God through the glasses of the revelation of His Word and a climactic revelation of Christ in Scripture has been for me a transforming experience. My daily prayer is that our God would be worshiped and adored for His perfections by all of His people throughout the world. In parts 3–6, the sidebar features entitled "Knowing Him" will offer practical ways to better know our God.

You *can* know Him. Equally important, you can continually grow in this knowledge of who God is (2 Peter 3:18). Such knowledge leads to joy (Psalm 89:16)! I pray that in some way my labor in writing this book enables me to be a "worker with you for your joy" (2 Corinthians 1:24) as you learn to ascribe to the Lord the glory due to His name (Psalm 29:2).

Note

1. Earl Radmacher, *You and Your Thoughts* (Wheaton: Tyndale, 1977), 41.

Part One

THE MOST FRUITFUL
INVESTMENT
OF YOUR LIFE

1

How Pursuing the Primary Thing— Knowing God—
RESULTS IN THE SECONDARY THINGS— THE DESIRES OF YOUR HEART

*H*OW DO YOU view yourself? Your perception of who you are affects your attitudes, thoughts, and actions around others. The greatest factor in how you view yourself is your perception of what the most important person in your life thinks of you.

That person's perception of you can be faulty, of course, but that doesn't immediately change your response to their words. The only way to let truth liberate you from lies that can cripple you is to embrace God as the most important Person in your life and listen to Him. He knows the truth. He created you.

Will you let Him speak truth to your spirit? Here are truths about you He declares in the Scriptures:

- "I accept you" (Romans 15:7).
- "You are a precious person to Me and I am continually thinking about you" (Psalm 139:17–18).
- "I'm continually devoted to you and will provide all that you need to fulfill My purpose for you" (Romans 8:31–32, 38–39).
- "I've adopted you into My family and will take care of you, lead you, discipline you, and develop you as your Father" (Galatians 4:5–6).
- "I'll live in you, and you'll never have to be alone as My Son, Jesus Christ, had to be when He died on the cross for you" (Galatians 2:20; Hebrews 13:5b).
- "I have a wonderful future for you, that you will know joy and satisfaction for all eternity" (Romans 8:18).
- "I have a unique plan of good works for you to accomplish" (Ephesians 2:10).
- "My plan is unique for you because no one else has your exact physical features, upbringing, talents, and abilities, and even your unique weaknesses" (Psalm 139:13–16).
- "I'll continue to work in you because My glory is at stake" (Philippians 2:13; Psalm 23:3).
- "I'll make you into a most attractive person in My eyes and allow you to fulfill My plan as you present your life to Me" (Romans 8:29; 12:1–2).

Let these truths from God uproot any lies that challenge His liberating truth. Use the shield of faith to knock down the lies that are thrown at you day by day.

Finding Real Meaning
and Purpose in Life

When we know God as He really is, we begin to know ourselves more accurately. And when we have a right relationship with Him, we understand our purpose for living. In fact, a significant purpose for living can be found only by being rightly related to our Creator — the One who created us for Himself (Colossians 1:16). Augustine is often quoted as saying, "Our hearts are restless until they find their rest in thee."

One who has real purpose has found someone worth dying for and worth living for. Since most of life is lived with a routine, a person with true purpose has found meaning even in the routines of life. God tells us that even the mundane — eating, drinking, or whatever we do — can be an opportunity to experience and display His glory (1 Corinthians 10:31). (The glory of God will be explored and explained in the final chapter of this book.)

A person with real meaning and purpose has learned the secret to overcoming boredom. Many gifted people with very "prestigious" jobs are bored and unfulfilled in their deepest longings. Why? They can do their job with a fraction of their God-given capacities — let's say 60 percent. They have a 40 percent boredom factor. God designed every part of our lives and bodies to be presented to Him (Romans 6:11–13; 12:1). God takes care of and uses what is presented to Him. He knows how to use every talent, gift, and ability we have. Even when a given task may not require all of our abilities, as we are yielded to Him, every part of our being can know His satisfying fellowship as we obey Him.

The True Meaning of Success

A person with real meaning and purpose has also come to grips with the true meaning of success. Success is finding, following, and fulfilling God's will for our life. The greatest statement of success ever written summarizes the life of the one perfect Person, Jesus. As the end of His life on earth approached, He said, "I glorified You on the earth, having accomplished the work which You have given Me to do" (John 17:4).

The apostle Paul encouraged others to follow him as he followed Christ. Look at his pursuit: "But I do not consider my life of any account as dear to myself, so that I may finish my course and the ministry which I received from the Lord Jesus, to testify solemnly of the gospel of the grace of God" (Acts 20:24). And look at his accomplishment: "I have fought the good fight, I have finished the course, I have kept the faith" (2 Timothy 4:7).

The Desire for Direction

Every human yearns to have direction. The breakthrough comes when we realize that we are a sheep in need of a divine shepherd to lead us (see Jeremiah 10:23). God leads us in His righteous paths in order to display to the world what a kind, merciful, and good shepherd He is (Psalm 23:3).

When there is a greater desire to know God's will than to know God, confusion will result. The thirst for direction is satisfied as one builds his life around the Shepherd.[1]

We are created by Christ and for Christ (Colossians 1:16). Our perfect Creator in His goodness desires us to experience the gift of enjoying Him. Since we are dependent creatures, when we live independent of Him, we must look to someone or something to attempt to meet the basic thirsts of our heart, including direction for our lives. The testimony of Scripture is consistent in describing the outcome of facing independently of God. Such independence results in *futility* (1 Samuel 12:21), *emptiness* (Jeremiah 2:5), *vanity* (Psalm 127:1-2), and *uselessness* (Romans 3:12).

Jesus summarized it by saying that "nothing" from God's eternal viewpoint can be accomplished independent of Him. "I am the vine, you are the branches; he who abides in Me and I in him, he bears much fruit, for apart from Me you can do nothing" (John 15:5).

The Desire for Contentment

How can a person really be free from the strain and pull of having to get ahead? How can one be free from being controlled by an unhealthy desire for status, possessions, and prestige? There is a secret—but it is an "open secret" that God has revealed to those who will look in His holy Word. The secret is learning to be content with what we have. Contentment is something that must be learned. No one is born with it, and only God can teach us to be content. However, contentment can be experienced in any circumstance in life. It is an attitude that the apostle Paul himself learned, no matter the circumstance:

Not that I speak from want, for I have learned to be content in whatever circumstances I am. I know how to get along with humble means, and I also know how to live in prosperity; in any and every circumstance I have learned the secret of being filled and going hungry, both of having abundance and suffering need. I can do all things through Him who strengthens me. (Philippians 4:11–13)

Notice how Paul alludes to a secret in verse 12 and reveals the secret in verse 13. The secret is our relationship to Christ. Paul wrote these words while in jail. He was behind bars, but he was also in Christ. Christ will give us the strength to do all that He has for us to do in any circumstance.

Listen to the psalmist's contentment: "Whom have I in heaven but You? And besides You, I desire nothing on earth" (Psalm 73:25). All we need to be content is knowing Christ is in heaven and chooses to provide what we need.

Let every longing for another person, position, or possession remind you of God's loving attention to you. That truth caused King David to declare:

How precious also are Your thoughts to me, O God!
How vast is the sum of them!
If I should count them, they would outnumber the sand.
When I awake, I am still with You. (Psalm 139:17–18)

When such longings come to you, recall Jesus' words to come to Him to quench your thirst:

Jesus stood and cried out, saying, "If anyone is thirsty, let him come to Me and drink. He who believes in Me, as the Scripture said, 'From his innermost being will flow rivers of living water.'" But this He spoke of the Spirit, whom those who believed in Him were to receive; for the Spirit was not yet given, because Jesus was not yet glorified. (John 7:37–39)

Few people ever meet a person who is truly at peace with himself. This kind of contentment is what frees one from selfish ambition and sets the person free to experience God's ambition for his life. Ask God to do this miracle in you!

The Desire for Security

The craving to be "in control" comes out of a knowledge that our self-interest will look after the people and things that we deem important. Are we really ever in control? Can we really completely control the decisions of others, the weather, the economy, or even our health? Our security must lie in being under the control of Another. One can find security in God because a believer in Christ can know these truths:

- "God is for us" (Romans 8:31).
- We cannot be separated from His love (see Romans 8:38–39).
- God's purposes cannot ultimately be defeated — even an unbeliever understood this (see Acts 5:38–39).
- God will guard all that I place in His hands (2 Timothy 1:12).

May this book aid you in finding a true delight in the Lord and as a by-product experience the deepest desires of your heart! I have shared the following prayer of dedication and trust with thousands of people. Would you be willing to pray this prayer in faith before you continue to read this book?

"God, I want to know You above all else in life. I need the motivation, encouragement, and wisdom to know how, but I desire it and want to desire it more. Give me the grace to repent of anything in

my life that is hindering my relationship to You. I believe You will overcome all obstacles and accomplish this in my life!
    "For Your name's sake and for my eternal benefit, Amen."

Note

1. See Bill Thrasher, *Living the Life God Has Planned: A Guide to Knowing God's Will* (Chicago: Moody, 2001), for further insight on this topic.

2

Why Study

THE CHARACTER
OF GOD?

$\mathscr{T}$HE APOSTLE PAUL tells us that a lack of the knowledge of God is shameful (1 Corinthians 15:34)! It is seen as the root of the moral problems of the human race (Hosea 4:1–2). The Bible says the basic problem and cause of man's rebellion is an absence of the fear of God (Romans 3:18), and an appropriate fear of God can be achieved only by having a knowledge of God.

Note how the fear of God and the knowledge of God are linked as parallel terms in Proverbs 2:5: "Then you will discern the fear of the Lord and discover the knowledge of God."

So by knowing the character of God we are able to properly respect and honor our Creator.

The One Who Reveals — and
The One who Distorts — God's Character

The "big idea" or central theme of the Bible is Christ (see Luke 24:27, 44; John 5:39), and Christ is the climax of the revelation of the character of God.

> God, after He spoke long ago to the fathers in the prophets in many portions and in many ways, in these last days has spoken to us in His Son, whom He appointed heir of all things, through whom also He made the world. And He is the radiance of His glory and the exact representation of His nature. (Hebrews 1:1–3a)

We are told to not be ignorant of Satan's schemes (2 Corinthians 2:11), and his primary scheme is the exact opposite of Christ's plan. The Devil wants to distort man's understanding of God's character. "Satan" means "adversary," and of course he opposes the primary aim of God's revelation. As a liar (John 8:44), he sought to plunge mankind into sin by lying to Eve about the goodness of God (Genesis 3:1–5). He uses the same tactic every day against all of mankind. We need to be ready by making our aim to know God and overcome the Devil's deceit through God's liberating truth.[1]

The Purpose of Creation and Redemption
Is for Man to Know God

We have been created by Christ and for Christ (Colossians 1:16). The world energized by Satan has rebelled against the Creator and offers a way of life independent of God. Everywhere we look we see men and women living their home lives, economic lives, vocational lives, recreational lives, and even their religious lives independent of God. If you had seen 1,000 lightbulbs in your life and over 900 of them were lying on the floor and less than 100 plugged into a socket, then that which is abnormal begins to look normal.

God's redemptive plan is to redeem us from the futility, vanity, and emptiness of a life independent of God (1 Peter 1:18). Eternal life is experientially knowing the true and living God and begins at the moment of salvation (John 17:3). God's design is for every person to enjoy His fellowship and presence in every facet of their life all the time.

The Key to Developing a Relationship with God Is a Right View of Him

To be sure, there is such a thing as a mere profession of knowing God that is at the same time being denied by the behavior of the professing believer (Titus 1:16). However, a genuine knowledge of God does lead to true understanding that will be reflected in a relationship with Him (Proverbs 9:10). Scripture speaks of both comprehending and knowing God (see Jeremiah 9:23–24). Table 1 on the following page shows the relationship between comprehending God and personalizing these truths so that you truly know God in your experience.

Jesus spoke of worshiping a God whom we know (John 4:22). The encouragement to press on to know the Lord is followed by the promise that we will be met by God's refreshment (Hosea 6:3). It is the true knowledge of God that will lead us to the experience of everything we need for life and godliness (2 Peter 1:3).

Table 1
Comprehending and Knowing God

Truths to Comprehend	Knowing God in Our Experience
Trustworthy[2]	Trust (Psalm 9:10; Hebrews 11:6)
Loving	Love (Matthew 22:36–40; John 14:15)
Delightful	Delight (Psalm 37:4)
Authority	Serve and Obey Him (Galatians 1:10; 1 Peter 5:6)
Perfection	Praise (Psalm 115:1–2; 1 Corinthians 10:31)

Notes

1. For insights into six of the most common symptoms of a wrong view of God, see Bill Thrasher, *Living the Life God Has Planned: A Guide to Knowing God's Will* (Chicago: Moody, 2001), 28–40.

2. For more insight on what it means to trust and delight in God, see Thrasher, *Living the Life God Has Planned*, 51–66.

Part Two

AN UNCHANGING, ETERNAL PERSON WHO CAN LIVE IN YOU

3

God Is Personable

HE IS NOT
SIMPLY AN INFLUENCE

PETER DEISON WRITES about Morris Davis, a suspected arsonist who was brought to the police station and subjected to a lie detector test. When he thought he was alone, he prayed, "Lord, let me get away with it, just this once." The problem was that the prayer was in the range of a policeman's hearing who later used it in the case against him. The ruling of the lower court was that since this was a private conversation, it could not be used as evidence.

This ruling was appealed and overturned, however, on the grounds that prayer cannot be considered a private conversation. Why? Because in the mind of the court, God is not a person. The headline of an American newspaper that reported the story was, "God Ruled a Non-Person."[1]

W. A. Criswell, former pastor of the First Baptist Church

of Dallas, Texas, was telling the story of Jesus asking His
disciples, "Who do men say that I am?" (see Matthew 16:13).
He made the observation that if Jesus were to come to a
group of modern philosophers and theologians, here is what
they might say: "Thou art the ground of being. Thou art the
leap of faith into the imperishable unknown. Thou art the exis-
tential, unphrasable, unverbalized, unpropositional, constan-
tation with the infinitude of inherent subjective experience."[2]
In the midst of all of our God-talk, we may discover that we
are finding it easier to talk about Him than truly relate to
Him on a personal level.

God Has the Attributes of Personality, and We Reflect His Divine Image

How does God reveal His personhood to us? The Scriptures indicate God has three elements of personality.

He has an intellect (Psalm 147:5). The Scriptures refer to the
thoughts and mind of the Lord (Isaiah 55:8, 1 Corinthians 2:16).

He has emotions (Psalm 18:19). We all think of God as love,
and so He is (see 1 John 4:8, 10). But God also is one who can
be grieved (see Ephesians 4:30) and who can experience
wrath (Romans 1:18). Similarly God the Son, Jesus, wept
(John 11:35), and the people around Him understood it as an
expression of His love (John 11:36).

He has a will (Ephesians 1:11). He makes predetermined
plans (Acts 2:23) and works all things together for the good
of His children who are called according to His purpose
(Romans 8:28–29).

Similarly, we have elements that reflect God's divine
image. When God the Father and God the Son created man
and woman, the Scriptures declare:

God said, "Let Us make man in Our image, according to Our likeness; and let them rule over the fish of the sea and over the birds of the sky and over the cattle and over all the earth, and over every creeping thing that creeps on the earth." God created man in His own image, in the image of God He created him; male and female He created them. (Genesis 1:26–27)

The account in Genesis 1 and 2 makes clear that He created Adam to reflect God's image. The Scriptures indicate Adam has three divine elements that ennoble him as a creature above all other created beings.

Adam demonstrates *an intellect*: God allowed him to name the animals, and in one afternoon, Adam named them all.

Adam has *emotions*: God provided Eve to be his companion to help the man with his fears and as well as the fulfillment of human companionship.

Adam has *a will*: God gave him a command to obey in the garden, which Adam (and his wife) could choose to obey — or disobey.

One aspect of being made in the image of God is that man has these three components of personality. God's gracious provision was for Adam to be able to express each of these capacities in fellowship with God.

God Performs Many Personal Functions

As you read Scriptures, you will encounter God performing the following personal functions. A good exercise in reading the Pentateuch (Genesis through Deuteronomy) or any of the major prophets (such as Isaiah or Ezekiel) is to note the many times God shows the following capacities:

- He speaks.
- He sees.
- He hears.
- He delights.
- He grieves.
- He desires.
- He sorrows.

God's supreme revelation of Himself was in the person of the Lord Jesus Christ. As the second person of the Trinity—God the Son—Jesus came to earth in human form, possessing both a divine and a human nature. The apostle John writes that Jesus is the supreme and climactic revelation of God (John 1:18; 14:9). The divine Son of God, incarnated in a village outside Jerusalem, demonstrated compassion, anger, weariness, and other emotions as He identified with the men and women He created (see Colossians 1:15–17).

Our Response to the Truth of God's Personhood

What is the correct response to the truth of God's personhood? It is that we can experience the greatness of God in a personal way.

We rejoice that we can find comfort in our relationship with Him. In fact, the greatness of God is not only that He knows everything but that you can say, "He knows *me!*" It is not only that He is sovereign over every event in the world but that He is intimately working in all of *your* concerns. It is not only that He loves the world but that He loves *you!*

The apostle Paul found comfort in an intimate, personal relationship with God the Son, who personally died for him: "I have been crucified with Christ; and it is no longer I who live, but Christ lives in *me*; and the life which I now live in the flesh I live by faith in the Son of God, who loved *me* and gave Himself up for *me*" (Galatians 2:20, italics added).

The fact that Jesus died on the cross is history, but experiencing the truth that He died for you is salvation. Our personal relationship with God is also captured by David in Psalm 31: "But as for me, I trust in You, O Lord, I say, 'You are *my* God'" (Psalm 31:14, italics added).

The Danger of Treating God Impersonally

Christians and non-Christians alike can fall into the trap of thinking of the almighty God as a distant, detached force, not the God who knows them and desires fellowship. The apostle Paul wrote with great urgency to the church of Galatia. The believers were being infiltrated with wrong ideas that told them that believing in Christ was only a first step in their salvation. False teachers were also arguing that the Galatian believers needed to submit to the ordinance of circumcision and pledge to keep the law in order to attain to their justification. Instead, those in Galatia needed to recall that God knew them personally and loved them. Paul wrote:

However at that time, when you did not know God, you were slaves to those which by nature are no gods. But now that you have come to know God, or rather to be known by God, how is it that you turn back again to the weak and worthless elemental things, to which you desire to be enslaved all over again? You observe days and months and seasons and years. I fear for you, that perhaps I have labored over you in vain. (Galatians 4:8–11)

Before they were saved, they did not know the true God. Salvation resulted in an intimate relationship with God that involved knowing God and being known by God. (Remember some people will hear these words on judgment day: "I never knew you" [Matthew 7:23]). Since they had tasted of the liberty of the relationship with God and now were turning back to their past bondage, Paul expressed great concern.

Has your Christian life degenerated into a ritual and a tradition? Is it only a conformity to a set of external ideas instead of a loving obedience to your heavenly Father? Ask God how you may be treating Him impersonally.

Developing a Friendship with God

Jesus' death has made it possible for the barrier of one's sin to be broken and for you to experience peace with God and stand in His favor (Romans 5:1–2). On the authority of God's Word, you can also develop a friendship with Christ. He told His followers that the responsibility of being His friend was to be a loyal servant who obeys Him (John 15:14). On His part, Jesus displayed His love for them as His friends not only by laying down His life for them (John 15:13) but also by not withholding any information they needed to know, and freely sharing God's truth with them (John 15:15). He made perfectly clear that He was the initiator of this friendship, which He intended would bear eternal benefits for them and others. He called this "fruit [that] would remain" (John 15:16).

This friendship can be such that one's greatest ambition

is to please Him. That was Paul's goal: "Therefore we also have as our ambition, whether at home or absent, to be pleasing to Him" (2 Corinthians 5:9).

Even when people call your actions a waste (see Mark 14:4) and even scold you (see Mark 14:5), your wonderful Lord can be so pleased as to call it a good deed (Mark 14:6) that will be remembered forever (Mark 14:9). For this reason a true disciple of Christ is to love Him supremely above all other relationships — even his own life (Matthew 10:37–39). You cannot please and love one who is not personable.

Leaning on Your Divine Helper

God has not only made possible a relationship with Him but has also given you a divine helper to make it possible for you to say with the psalmist, "You are my God" (Psalm 31:14). The Holy Spirit will foster and develop this intimate relationship: "Because you are sons, God has sent forth the Spirit of His Son into our hearts, crying, 'Abba! Father!'" (Galatians 4:6).

It is the Spirit who enables the believer to address our God as "Abba! Father!" As Donald Campbell observes,

The word "Abba" is the Aramaic word for father. It is the diminutive form used by small children in addressing their fathers. It is appropriate to see its similarity to the English word "Daddy" used by Christ (cf. Mark 14:36). This familiar form indicates intimacy and trust as opposed to the formality of legalism.[3]

One of the privileges of having God as our heavenly Father is to experience the leading of the Holy Spirit (Romans

8:14). A careful meditation upon the three verses that follow Romans 8:14 reveals much about what the Spirit desires to lead you to experience.

Verse 15 tells us that *God's Spirit wants to lead you into freedom.* We know this because "you have not received a spirit of slavery . . ." (v. 15). We do not even know what freedom is — much less how to experience it without the Spirit's help.

God's Spirit also wants to lead you into facing and overcoming your paralyzing fears. "For you have not received a spirit of slavery leading to fear again" (v. 15). God wants you to admit your unhealthy fears, seek Him at each point of fear, and experience His deliverance (Psalm 34:4).[4]

God's Spirit desires to lead you into intimacy with God. We can take wonderful spiritual disciplines and yet not arrive at the intimacy of God without the Spirit's motivation and enablement. We need His help. Recall the promise of Galatians 4:6: "God has sent forth the Spirit of His Son into our hearts, crying, 'Abba! Father!'" In Romans 8:15 the apostle Paul assures us, "You have received a spirit of adoption as sons by which we cry out, 'Abba! Father!'" And as Campbell observes, the word *Abba* "indicates intimacy and trust."[5]

God's Spirit desires to lead you into assurance. You need to be assured of things you already know. You can know a truth and still can learn it at a deeper level of assurance. Romans 8 tells us the Holy Spirit gives such assurance: "The Spirit Himself testifies with our spirit that we are children of God" (v. 16). God wants you to not only know that you have a loving heavenly Father; He wants you to be filled, or controlled, by this truth.

The God of Hope

Finally, *God's Spirit desires to lead you into a life of hope.* Romans 8 also assures us that as children of God, we are "heirs of God and fellow heirs with Christ, if indeed we suffer with Him so that we may also be glorified with Him" (v. 17). God is a "God of hope" and desires that "you will abound in hope by the power of the Holy Spirit" (Romans 15:13). In a world that offers a false hope and promotes despair, God desires that such hope may overflow from us to others.

The late Ruth Bell Graham, author and wife of evangelist Billy Graham, grew up as the daughter of a missionary surgeon in China. She attended a boarding school in North Korea in the 1930s. When the time came for her mother and father to send her away, the anticipated parting was so painful for Ruth that she prayed that she would die. Morning came, and she was still alive; so she grabbed her bags and said good-bye to her parents, her Chinese friends, fellow missionaries, and her home.

Even after a week, she experienced no relief from her homesickness. The nights were particularly hard, and she would drown her pillow with tears night after night. After becoming ill and finding no relief from her pain, she had a conversation with her older sister Rosa, who was also enrolled at the boarding school. Rosa told her to take some verse and put her own name on the verse and see if that would help. Ruth turned to her favorite chapter, Isaiah 53, and began to follow this Spirit-led advice. She began to meditate in this way: "He was pierced through for Ruth's transgressions; He was crushed for Ruth's iniquities." As she continued this exercise, her heart leaped and the healing of her homesickness began! She was experiencing her personal God.[6]

Like Ruth Graham that day nearly eighty years ago, may you experience your personal God this very day.

Notes

1. Peter V. Deison, *The Priority of Knowing God* (Grand Rapids: Kregel, 2000), 22.

2. As quoted by a former student of mine and attributed to Dr. Criswell.

3. Donald Campbell, "Galatians," in the *Bible Knowledge Commentary New Testament Edition* (Wheaton, Ill.: Victor, 1983), 601.

4. For more insight into dealing with unhealthy fears, see Bill Thrasher, *How to Be a Soul Physician* (Seattle: CreateSpace, 2010), 239–58. The book can be found at the author's website, www.victoriouspraying.com.

5. Campbell, "Galatians," 601.

6. Robert J. Morgan, *On This Day: 365 Amazing and Inspiring Stories about Saints, Martyrs & Heroes* (Nashville: Nelson, 1997), September 2.

4

God Is Spirit

BUT HE
CAN BE KNOWN

*G*OD'S ESSENTIAL NATURE is spirit (John 4:24). None has seen the invisible essence of God (John 1:18). He has at times given visible manifestations of Himself, which are known as theophanies. He has also revealed His invisible attributes, and the climax of this revelation was in Jesus Christ. Jesus is said to be the "image of the invisible God" (Colossians 1:15) and the "exact representation of His nature" (Hebrews 1:3).

How do you get to know one who is invisible? You get to know Him by faith. "Faith is . . . the conviction of things not seen" (Hebrews 11:1). In fact, as you behold the revelation of His attributes, you will be transformed (2 Corinthians 3:18)! We eagerly anticipate the day that when He appears we will "see Him just as He is" (1 John 3:2), "face to face" (1 Corinthians 13:12), and then we will be like Him!

However, even now, though we have not seen Him, we can love Him, trust Him, and find our joy in Him. As Peter wrote, "And though you have not seen Him, you love Him, and though you do not see Him now, but believe in Him, you greatly rejoice with joy inexpressible and full of glory, obtaining as the outcome of your faith the salvation of your souls" (1 Peter 1:8–9).

Use of Anthropomorphisms

God is spirit and has graciously chosen to reveal Himself to us. He uses language associated with the human body to reveal to us His capacities that relate to these physical parts of man. An anthropomorphism is an expression that gives God human or personal characteristics. In the Scriptures God is described as having eyes, a hand, a mouth, and various other human elements. Thus the prophet Hanani told King Asa of Judah, "For the eyes of the Lord move to and fro throughout the earth that He may strongly support those whose heart is completely His" (2 Chronicles 16:9).

This shows God's awareness and knowledge of all people and events on the earth to support anyone who looks to Him and Him alone. The context reveals that Asa was not such a man because of his reliance on the king of Aram.

The prophet Isaiah tells God's people of God's power and ability to hear His people by giving God a hand and an ear: "Behold, the Lord's hand is not so short that it cannot save; nor is His ear so dull that it cannot hear" (Isaiah 59:1).

His hand represents God's power to act, and His ear God's attentiveness and ability to listen. The problem is not with His capacities but rather with the unrepentant sin that has separated His people from their holy God. Earlier the

Lord had previewed the blessed outcome for His people if they would obey His Sabbath command:

> If because of the sabbath, you turn your foot from doing your own pleasure on My holy day, and call the sabbath a delight, the holy day of the Lord honorable, and honor it, desisting from your own ways, from seeking your own pleasure and speaking your own word, then you will take delight in the Lord, and I will make you ride on the heights of the earth; and I will feed you with the heritage of Jacob your father, for the *mouth* of the Lord has spoken. (Isaiah 58:13–14, italics added)

His mouth represents His ability to speak and make promises to which He will be absolutely faithful.

As his career approached an end, Moses urged the people to honor and trust God. He drew a picture of a mighty yet protective God as he described the "arms" of God: "The eternal God is a dwelling place, and underneath are the everlasting arms; and He drove out the enemy from before you, and said, 'Destroy!'" (Deuteronomy 33:27).

Moses speaks of His arms that will support and protect His people as well as be active in fighting against their enemies.

Jesus, who knew the Father intimately in heaven as well as while on earth, drew a picture of a God who held Christ's followers secure when He said: "My Father, who has given them to Me, is greater than all; and no one is able to snatch them out of the Father's hand" (John 10:29). God's all-powerful hand speaks of His ability to secure His people so that they have nothing to fear.

David describes the fierceness of God in two vivid verses in 2 Samuel 22:

Smoke went up out of His *nostrils*, fire from His *mouth* devoured; coals were kindled by it. (v. 9)

Then the channels of the sea appeared, the foundations of the world were laid bare by the rebuke of the Lord, at the blast of the breath of His *nostrils*. (v. 16, all italics added)

The idea is that of violently breathing, which is symptomatic of the expression of His righteous judgment. The smoke is the forerunner of His judgment—fire.

Moses enjoyed an intimate level of friendship with God, described this way in Exodus 33:11: "Thus the Lord used to speak to Moses face to face, just as a man speaks to his friend. When Moses returned to the camp, his servant Joshua, the son of Nun, a young man, would not depart from the tent" (Exodus 33:11).

But this does not mean Moses actually gazed upon the glory and essence of God. When he requested that God reveal His glory, God declined (vv. 18–20), saying, "You cannot see My *face*, for no man can see Me and live!"

Moses' request, "I pray You, show me Your glory" goes beyond the intimate experience that he enjoyed with God. Though he viewed some manifestation of God, what this visible representation was is not precisely revealed. We do know that no one has seen His face, which here speaks of His invisible essence (John 1:18; 6:46; 1 Timothy 1:17; 1 John 4:12).

The Blessing of God
Being a Spirit Being

God is spirit. You might say, "I need a person with a body right next to me." Remember that He did send His Son in a body, and He also has His church, the body of Christ, to represent Him now.

You can also praise Him that He is spirit. He is not limited with a body that can be in only one place at a time. God is not bound in this way. He is not a limited geographical deity. "He is absolutely free from all limitations of space and time," B. F. Westcott reminds us.[1] As spirit, He is present in all places at all times. You need more than a person right next to you. You need one who can live *inside* of you!

Jesus spoke of one's "innermost being" (John 7:38). It is this innermost being that only God as spirit can satisfy. Only He can fully quench your thirst. You have needs that are beyond what another human being can meet. Even a "perfect" job, "perfect" mate, or "perfect" vacation can leave you less than satisfied. Only God who is spirit is able to live inside of you to quench your thirst.

Jesus spoke of this inner thirsting of our spirit during the last day of the Feast of Tabernacles in Jerusalem. There

> Jesus stood and cried out, saying, "If anyone is thirsty, let him come to Me and drink. He who believes in Me, as the Scripture said, 'From his innermost being will flow rivers of living water.'" But this He spoke of the Spirit, whom those who believed in Him were to receive. (John 7:37–39)

Jesus is saying that He alone can satisfy our thirst as we keep coming to Him in faith. Praise Him that if you know Christ, He is not any distance from you but lives inside of you and is eager to listen to your cries.

Worshiping God in Spirit

Speaking to a Samaritan woman one afternoon, Jesus declared, "An hour is coming, and now is, when the true worshipers will worship the Father in spirit and truth; for such people the Father seeks to be His worshipers. God is spirit, and those who worship Him must worship in spirit and truth" (John 4:23–24).

The fact that God is spirit demands that He be worshiped in spirit and truth (John 4:24). The "must" in John 4:24 speaks of divine necessity and not just something desirable. It is the same force that you see in John 3:7 — "you *must* be born again" — and in John 3:14, when Jesus declares, "Even so *must* the Son of Man be lifted up" (italics added).

Jesus spoke of "true worshipers" (John 4:23). True worshipers respond to the true God (John 17:3) who seeks worshipers.

If you were perfect in every way, the greatest gift you could give someone would be the ability to enjoy you as you are! God is perfect in every way and not in need of anything or anyone. In His love He desires to allow you and me to enjoy Him in worship.

What does it mean to worship in spirit? The first interpretive decision to make is to determine whether Jesus is talking about the Holy Spirit or the human spirit. The context seems to reveal that the word "spirit" in John 4:23–24 is referring to spiritual worship in response to the question of the place of worship (see John 4:21–24). To be sure, this kind of worship is in response to the Holy Spirit. It is the filling of the Spirit (Ephesians 5:18) that results in true worship (Ephesians 5:19–20). To worship in spirit is to worship from our heart or inner being. Jesus spoke of people who honored

God with their lips, but their hearts were far away from Him (Matthew 15:8). Charles Spurgeon used to say, "If our hearts have not sung, we have not sung and worship has not taken place. God listens to our hearts."

To "worship in spirit" is to let the true you speak to the true God. It is the awesome privilege of coming to Him with your fears (Psalm 34:4), anxieties (Philippians 4:6-7), need for cleansing (1 John 1:7-9), true desires (Psalm 37:4), and temptations (Hebrews 4:15-16). God's people were not to let their true lives hide behind their external worship.[2]

When we worship in spirit, God tells us that these are appropriate sacrifices that the believer can offer.

- A broken and contrite heart (Psalm 51:16-17)
- The presentation of our bodies (Romans 12:1)
- The fruit of our ministry (Romans 15:16)
- Financial gifts to God's servants (Philippians 4:18)
- Praise and thanksgiving (Hebrews 13:15)
- Doing good and sharing (Hebrews 13:16)
- Prayer (Revelation 5:8; 8:3-4)

The Father is seeking worshipers who respond to the Holy Spirit and offer such sacrifices.

Worshiping God in Truth

To worship in spirit is to worship with "complete sincerity," and to worship in truth is to worship in "complete reality."[3] An idol is that which a person looks to in order to meet the thirst of their heart. If one rejects God, we will look to an idol and in so doing "[exchange] the truth of God for a lie" (Romans 1:25). To worship in truth is to worship the one

"true God" (John 17:3) in line with God's first command-
ment, "You shall have no other gods before Me" (Exodus
20:3).

Table 2 Free to Worship the True God	
Free from Lies	**Free to Worship in Truth**
A god who is harsh	A God who is gracious
A god who tolerates sin	A God who is holy
A god who is stingy	A God who is generous
A god who is distant and indifferent	A God who is intimate and caring
A god who is insensitive to pain	A God who is understanding and merciful

There is no truth in the Devil, who is "a liar and the father
of lies" (John 8:44). He lusts for worship and one day will
empower the antichrist, who will demand that people worship Satan (2 Thessalonians 2:4; Revelation 13:4). Even now
the Devil sows lies to distract you from the worship of the
true God.

Because truth is in Jesus (John 1:14; 14:6), worshiping in
truth will always lead you to Him. We can depend upon the
"Spirit of truth" to guide us into the worship of Christ (John
16:13–15). His truth sets one free (John 8:32), and worshiping
in truth will set us free to worship God as He has revealed
Himself.

God is spirit and those who worship Him must worship
in spirit and truth (John 4:24).

Notes

1. B. F. Westcott, *The Gospel According to Saint John* (Grand Rapids: Eerd-mans, 1975), 73.

2. For the abuse of worship, see 1 Samuel 13:8–14; Psalm 50:7–15; Isaiah 48:1–2; 59:3–5; Amos 5:21–27; Micah 6:6–8.

3. Leon Morris, *The Gospel According to John* (Grand Rapids: Eerdmans, 1971), 271.

5

God Is Immutable

HE IS UNCHANGING

*I*N A WORLD that is changing at a record pace, it is comforting to be able to build your life around a God who does not change. A student who studied at the seminary I attended had transferred from another school. The brand of liberal theology that he had previously studied was a passing fad, and by the time he graduated even the professors at that seminary no longer believed it. He had a salvation experience and now was studying in a seminary that believed in an unchanging God. This God had given a revelation of Himself that would never go out-of-date.

This is the God revealed in the Bible. No greater passage than Psalm 102 declares the truth that God does not and cannot change.

Of old You founded the earth, and the heavens are the work of Your hands. Even they will perish, but You endure; and all of them will wear out like a garment; like clothing You will change them and they will be changed. But You are the same, and Your years will not come to an end. The children of Your servants will continue, and their descendants will be established before You. (Psalm 102:25–28)

James the apostle describes God the Father as lacking in any variation: "Every good thing given and every perfect gift is from above, coming down from the Father of lights, with whom there is no variation or shifting shadow" (James 1:17).

His Immutability Testifies to His Perfection

Theologians call this constancy and lack of change *immutability*. God is unchangeable. He is immutable. Would you like to be immutable? If you are in any way cognizant of your shortcomings, you would emphatically say, "No, I can't do that! That's not me; I'm not consistent. I don't have my life together like that."

God's immutability testifies to His perfection. He does not need to mature in any of His qualities. He could not possibly be wiser, more loving, more merciful, or more holy. Every quality is in its perfected state. Likewise, He does not need to add any quality to make Him more complete. God states that the fruit of responding correctly to trials is Christlike character. He describes this as being both "perfect and complete" (James 1:4). God's character is such that not only is each quality perfect, but also He (unlike us) is not missing any perfection. He is perfectly balanced in all His perfections, unlike the man who is generous but also wasteful or the one who is frugal but also stingy. God has *every* quality — He is complete — and each quality is in its highest perfection.

Because God is immutable, He is not running out of any of His qualities. You may have been in a great trial and cried out to Him for deliverance. After God grants you deliverance, He does not have any less power to do it for you or anyone else the next time. You do not burden Him down or wear Him out by casting your cares upon His shoulders. You can see Him richly bless another person out of His kindness and goodness. When you are tempted to be jealous, remember that He has no less kindness and goodness left over for you. He is immutable in His goodness, and it is not being depleted.

His Immutability Applies to All His Attributes

I remember one time feeling very encouraged as I sensed God's love for me. Then I reminded myself, *This is* always *His attitude toward me as His child.* Unfortunately, you and I often interpret His love for us based on our emotional state, which often is influenced by our present circumstances. Instead we should base our confidence on His unchangeable truth that says we cannot be separated from His love (Romans 8:38–39).

All of His attributes are immutable. He has known, does know, and always will know all things. He is truthful, and His Word is forever "settled in heaven" (Psalm 119:89), "stands forever" (Isaiah 40:8), and "cannot be broken" (John 10:35). His holiness and love are always just as intense as when Jesus was dying on the cross for us!

One day a radio listener sent the following poem to a

radio pastor. I have shared it with thousands of people. It relates to God's unchanging faithfulness.

> Yesterday God helped me
> Today He will do the same.
> How long will it last?
> Forever, praise His name!

Hope for the Repentant

How are the passages that say that God has changed His mind or relented to be interpreted? For example, many stumble over God's decision to withhold punishment on wicked Nineveh once the people of the city repented. The prophet Jonah could not understand it and was frustrated with God. Here's how the book of Jonah describes God's actions: "When God saw their deeds, that they turned from their wicked way, then God relented concerning the calamity which He had declared He would bring upon them. And He did not do it" (Jonah 3:10).

The truths of His sovereignty, faithfulness, and loving compassion do not change. However, God has an unchanging faithfulness to His Word. He enters into relationship with changing men and women. He has always promised to bless a repentant heart and judge an unrepentant heart.

At one moment I might speak concerning a nation or concerning a kingdom to uproot, to pull down, or to destroy it; if that nation against which I have spoken turns from its evil, I will relent concerning the calamity I planned to bring on it. Or at another moment I might speak concerning a nation or concerning a kingdom to build up or to plant it; if it does evil in My sight by not obeying My voice, then I will think better of the good with which I had promised to bless it. (Jeremiah 18:7–10)

These verses in no way contradict this attribute but rather affirm it! Mankind is under judgment; the sentence has been set for our sins. Yet God will change His judgment as we acknowledge our wrongs, no matter what point in our life, no matter what our sins, whether we are rich and famous or poor and seemingly ordinarily. Mickey Mantle, the famous New York Yankees baseball player, repented and professed Christ at the end of his life. He was led to the Lord by his teammate Bobby Richardson, who had faithfully served Christ for many years. After his conversion, Mantle said to his fans, "Don't be like me, I'm no role model!" He realized he had not been a role model in his life.[1]

How to Feel Secure

What is the basis of your security? Most of the time we look to one of these four things to meet our need for security: *people, positions, possessions,* or *practices.*

You and I have a need to feel secure; God has placed that need in each of our hearts. Ultimately this need can be met only by an unchanging God. This is why one of the kindest commands in all of Scripture is the command to have no other gods before Him (Exodus 20:3). The four wrong bases for security are also the four directions that our heart flows into idolatry. Do you see the obvious insecurity that this brings?

- *People.* People may change. Your good friend may be moody, unresponsive, unreceptive to you — or may even die and no longer be available.

- *Positions.* Circumstances can change. What once was so ideal now may suddenly be something totally different. You may also lose a position that once met your need for security.
- *Possessions.* God's word even to a rich person is to not "fix their hope on the uncertainty of riches" (1 Timothy 6:17). Possessions are things that are to lead us to God who "richly supplies us with all things to enjoy" (1 Timothy 6:17). Even an abundance of possessions cannot satisfy or bring security. They are at best only temporary provisions.
- *Practices.* When you base your security on what you do rather than on God and what He has done, you are on shaky ground. The simple fact is that you are trusting in yourself rather than in God, and "he who trusts in his own heart is a fool" (Proverbs 28:26).

All four of these bases of security are unreliable and clearly changeable. Build your life around the One who does not change!

Guidance for Our Lives

As we behold God's glory, we will be transformed into the glory of Christ's likeness (2 Corinthians 3:18; Romans 8:29). To be sure, we are not immutable, but we are to let God build steadfastness into our lives. The Scripture urges us to "be steadfast, immovable, always abounding in the work of the Lord, knowing that your toil is not in vain in the Lord" (1 Corinthians 15:58).

We are to trust in God's immutable faithfulness. As we do, He will transform us into faithful men and women, who are instructed to "be faithful until death." Even if our faithfulness costs us our lives, we know the faithful, unchanging God sustains us to the end. And a reward awaits for our faithfulness: "Be faithful until death, and I will give you the crown of life" (Revelation 2:10).

Rest in His unchanging character and lean on His Spirit to transform you into a steadfast and faithful person. He will be faithful to supply you with whatever you need to be faithful in your relationships, job, and service. Trust your immutable God one day at a time.

Note

1. Ed Cheek, "Mickey Mantle: His Final Inning," tract of the American Tract Society, 1998. Mantle battled alcoholism for forty years, but his life is a testimony that God will honor the repentance of those who cry out to Him.

6

God Is Eternal
FROM EVERLASTING
TO EVERLASTING HE IS GOD

*G*OD IS INFINITE in relation to time. There never was a time when He did not exist and never will be a time when He does not exist. Moses said it well in the book of Psalms:

> Before the mountains were born or You gave birth to the
> earth and the world,
> Even from everlasting to everlasting, You are God.
> (Psalm 90:2)

All of us have been created by an eternal God. None of us can escape the urge that He has put in our hearts—the desire to be connected with someone who is eternal—because He has set eternity in our hearts (Ecclesiastes 3:11).

The Desire for Lasting Significance

It is painful to envision a life that is only like building a sand castle that will get washed away when the next high wave splashes upon the shore. For this reason most of us try to keep busy enough to escape this tormenting thought. We choose to pay big money for entertainment that promises to deaden the pain of our insignificance. Choosing to believe the lies of our culture, we trust and even glory in our temporal possessions with the illusion that they will last forever.

The psalmist testifies to this when he writes: "Their inner thought is that their houses are forever and their dwelling places to all generations; they have called their lands after their own names. But man in his pomp will not endure; he is like the beasts that perish" (Psalm 49:11–12). He goes on to give this advice against building our lives around temporal things: "Do not be afraid when a man becomes rich, when the glory of his house is increased; for when he dies he will carry nothing away; his glory will not descend after him" (49:16–17).

Those Things That Endure

Many things pass with the end of our earthly lives. Does anything endure? In the Scriptures, our never-ending, incorruptible God says yes. One day I was studying the verse that describes how man, in rejecting God, "exchanged the glory of the incorruptible God for an image in the form of corruptible man . . ." (Romans 1:23). This verse prompted me to ask a question, "How many things in Scripture does God describe as incorruptible?" I discovered that the Greek word translated "incorruptible" (and in other verses "imperishable") describes five things in the Scriptures.

1. God: "The glory of the *incorruptible* God" (Romans 1:23, all italics added). God remains forever, from eternity past into eternity future.
2. His Word: "born again not of seed which is perishable but *imperishable*, that is, through the living and enduring word of God" (1 Peter 1:23). Spoken to the prophets millennia ago, God's holy Word remains today, despite efforts of kings and despots to ban, even destroy, copies of the Bible.
3. Godly character: "the *imperishable* quality of a gentle and quiet spirit, which is precious in the sight of God" (1 Peter 3:4). God approves of a humble spirit, one founded on Him and thus enduring in nature.
4. Resurrected body: "For this perishable must put on the imperishable, and this mortal must put on immortality" (1 Corinthians 15:53). Every man and woman will die, but there is judgment and life after death (Hebrews 9:27). The saints (followers of Jesus) will live forever with Him in heaven, with perfect bodies that will neither die nor suffer attack by disease or aging.
5. Eternal rewards: "Everyone who competes in the games exercises self-control in all things. They then do it to receive a perishable wreath, but we an *imperishable*" (1 Corinthians 9:25). God will reward His faithful followers for their enduring accomplishments on behalf of His kingdom.

Notice how these five incorruptible things speak to us about a correct philosophy of life. We could state this philosophy in this way: "Build your life around *God* and His *Word*. Let Him build godly *character* in your life as you anticipate your *resurrected* body and eternal *rewards*."

Why Have an Eternal Perspective?

Jesus, the incarnate revelation of the eternal God, taught His followers four key truths about having an eternal perspective on life. Though it may be a challenge to look beyond the present day with its demands for our time, a true perspective on life should focus on eternity. Here are four truths that should give us an eternal focus:

First, an eternal gain is better than a temporal gain. "Do not store up for yourselves treasures on earth, where moth and rust destroy, and where thieves break in and steal. But store up for yourselves treasures in heaven, where neither moth nor rust destroys, and where thieves do not break in or steal" (Matthew 6:19–20).

Only what is eternal will last beyond this life.

Second, a temporal loss is better than an eternal loss. "If your right eye makes you stumble, tear it out and throw it from you; for it is better for you to lose one of the parts of your body, than for your whole body to be thrown into hell. If your right hand makes you stumble, cut it off and throw it from you; for it is better for you to lose one of the parts of your body, than for your whole body to go into hell" (Matthew 5:29–30).

Do you reflect each day on the brevity of this life? There are only two destinations—heaven or hell. You and every person you know will go to one or the other for all eternity.

Third, sacrifices you make for Christ will be eternally rewarded. Jesus said, "Everyone who has left houses or brothers or sisters or father or mother or children or farms for My name's sake, will receive many times as much, and will inherit eternal life" (Matthew 19:29).

His evaluation of our life is all that will ultimately matter.

Fourth, the key to eternal significance is abiding in Christ. As Jesus told His disciples, "I am the vine, you are the branches; he who abides in Me and I in him, he bears much fruit, for apart from Me you can do nothing" (John 15:5).

Jesus says the way to eternal significance is to know Him and lean on His strength in us. Paul the apostle says the same thing in Philippians 4:13, attributing any lasting accomplishment to the Christ who strengthens him. Any accomplishments not empowered and motivated by Christ will be eternally vain (Psalm 127:1-2).

A Relationship with the Eternal God Gives Us a Perspective on Who We Are

When we have a relationship with the eternal God, granted by being children of God through our belief in Jesus Christ (John 1:12), there are many benefits. We begin with our perspective about who we are on earth. We are "citizens of heaven" (Philippians 3:20) and are to be eagerly waiting for our Lord to come take us to our eternal home in heaven (John 14:1-3). We are "aliens and strangers" in this world and should not be surprised that we do not really feel at home (1 Peter 2:11). We are here on official business as "ambassadors for Christ" (2 Corinthians 5:20).

Life on this earth is very brief and compared to a "vapor" that appears for a short time and then vanishes away (James 4:14).

Yet as children of God, we can easily lose this perspective of who we are. Daily we need to remind ourselves that this world is not our home. We must remember that we entered this world with nothing: "Naked I came from my mother's womb" (Job 1:21), and we "cannot take anything out of it either" (1 Timothy 6:7). As has often been said, you will never see a U-Haul trailer full of things behind the hearse that carries the dead body to the grave. We are here to do the eternal will of our God and abide in Him each moment of the day.

A Relationship with the Eternal God Gives Us a Perspective on Time

It is rare that a youth grasps the value of time and the brevity of life. The events of the day, their energy and vitality, and anticipation of the upcoming week can make teens think there are no limits to their earthly lives. Similarly, many adults, caught up in the tyranny of urgent things or even planning for a future vacation, will target the here-and-now, forgetting their life here is short. Eternity should be their focus.

One of the changes that God worked in me after I surrendered my life to Him was my view of time. I agree with writer Richard Polle: "It is a serious waste to let a day go by without allowing God to change us."[1] We all live under the command to make the most of our time (Ephesians 5:16). As Lawrence Scupoli puts it, "God has granted you the morning, but He does not promise the evening. Spend each day as if it were your last."[2]

God has given each of us the time we need to do His will. Jesus said this at the end of His short earthly life: "I glorified You on the earth, having accomplished the work which You have given Me to do" (John 17:4).

Moses was an older man when he penned this prayer: "So teach us to number our days, that we may present to You a heart of wisdom" (Psalm 90:12). Most of us may not like deadlines but would agree that they help us to get things done. In Psalm 90:10 Moses gives a general rule regarding the span of our earthly lives — seventy or eighty years. Of course, one's life could be much briefer or could be longer.

Over thirty years ago, I took Moses' prayer of Psalm 90:10 and literally began to number my days. I counted the number of days a person has if he lives seventy years by multiplying 70 by 365.25. I then subtracted the number of days I had already lived based on my age at that time. For the past thirty-plus years, I have put a new number at the top of each day in my Day-Timer — one lower than the day before. To be certain, each day could be my last and could also be the day that our wonderful Lord returns to get His children. My number is much lower now than it was thirty-plus years ago. Each of us needs to realize the great gift of the brief time that God has given us to live on this earth for our eternal God. As Jesus said, "Night is coming when no man can work" (John 9:4). Why not pray Moses' prayer of Psalm 90:12 for yourself?

Even with an eternal perspective, sometimes it is hard to wait patiently and trust God's timing in our lives. However, many times God will appoint waiting as a prelude to a special blessing that He has for you. Such waiting lets Him do a special work in and through our lives as we wait.[3]

A Relationship with the Eternal God Gives Us a Perspective on Trials

Businessman Walter Petherick took his four children to church one evening during the London Plague of 1665. The minister read Habakkuk 3:17–18.

> Though the fig tree should not blossom and there be no fruit on the vines, though the yield of the olive should fail and the fields produce no food, though the flock should

be cut off from the fold and there be no cattle in the stalls, yet I will exult in the Lord, I will rejoice in the God of my salvation. (Habakkuk 3:17–18)

After the widower sent his children to bed, he cried in repentance for being more concerned for figs, olives, and cattle than the things of the Lord. His spirit was reborn and he found peace with God.

When the great fire consumed London the next year and threatened Petherick's warehouse, this time he met the trial with great trust and in peace submitted all his belongings to the Lord, purposing to rejoice in God no matter what! In this case his children and his warehouse were mercifully spared.[4]

We cannot trust God with any trial unless we first put it in perspective. Scripture frequently tells us we can handle our trials only when we place them in the perspective of eternity. Consider these three passages:

For I consider that the sufferings of this present time are not worthy to be compared with the glory that is to be revealed to us. (Romans 8:18)

For momentary, light affliction is producing for us an eternal weight of glory far beyond all comparison, while we look not at the things which are seen, but at the things which are not seen; for the things which are seen are temporal, but the things which are not seen are eternal. (2 Corinthians 4:17–18)

In this you greatly rejoice, even though now for a little while, if necessary, you have been distressed by various trials, so that the proof of your faith, being more precious than gold which is perishable, even though tested by fire, may be found to result in praise and glory and honor at the revelation of Jesus Christ. (1 Peter 1:6–7)

All of us need a glimpse of heaven that enables us to put this life in perspective. We must listen carefully to the Scriptures that encourage us not to get caught up in this world but rather to "fix [our] hope *completely* on the grace to be brought to [us] at the revelation of Jesus Christ" (1 Peter 1:13, italics added). In the preface to his classic book *Heaven*, Randy Alcorn gives the following insightful illustration.

Young Florence Chadwick had been the first woman to swim the English channel both ways. Now she entered the waters of the Pacific Ocean off Catalina Island, determined to swim the twenty-six miles to the mainland California. The foggy and chilly weather made the route discouraging, and she could hardly see the boats accompanying her. Yet she continued to swim fifteen hours, seemingly making good progress.

But the weather and lack of vision were taking their toll. At one point she begged to be taken out of the water. Her mother spoke through the fog from a nearby boat; she told Florence she was close and that she could make it. The weary swimmer continued, not sure where she was.

Finally, physically and emotionally exhausted, [Florence] stopped swimming and was pulled out. It wasn't until she was on the boat that she discovered the shore was less than half a mile away. At a news conference the next day she said, "All I could see was the fog . . . I think if I could have seen the shore, I would have made it."[5]

If only Florence could have seen beyond her present condition to what waited just beyond.

Similarly, if we can place the trial in perspective, we often
can see the eternal benefits of the current unpleasant situation. (For example, see Psalm 73 for how perspective transformed the attitude of the psalmist.) A Puritan writer once
said that if someone threw you a bag of gold and it knocked
you out as you reached out to catch it, you would not rebuke
the person for giving you the gold after you awoke. Trials are
like that. They temporarily may knock you out, but they also
enrich your soul. Here are some of the ways that trials can
enrich our life.

1. They give you a special opportunity to experience
   Christ's peace. Jesus spoke so that "in Me you may
   have peace. In the world you have tribulation, but take
   courage; I have overcome the world" (John 16:33).
2. They will enlarge your capacity to experience Christ's
   joy. In 2 Corinthians 8:2 we read of God's people experiencing an "abundance of joy" in the midst of a "great
   ordeal of affliction" (see also John 16:20–22).
3. They will give you an opportunity to know the God of
   all comfort and the Father of mercies (2 Corinthians 1:3).[6]
4. They will enhance your ability to minister. Paul told the
   believers in the church at Corinth that the comfort of
   God in the midst of their pain would enable them to
   comfort others. "[God] comforts us in all our affliction
   so that we will be able to comfort those who are in any
   affliction with the comfort with which we ourselves
   are comforted by God" (2 Corinthians 1:4).
5. They will give you an opportunity to learn new lessons
   of faith. That's what Paul learned. "In Asia . . . we were

burdened excessively, beyond our strength, so that we despaired even of life; indeed, we had the sentence of death within ourselves so that we would not trust in ourselves, but in God who raises the dead" (2 Corinthians 1:8–9).

6. They will build perseverance in your life. The apostle James declares "the testing of your faith produces endurance" (James 1:3).

7. They will give you opportunities for ministry and evangelism. Paul knew that trials could be useful in the midst of hard ministry, telling young Timothy, "I endure all things for the sake of those who are chosen, so that they also may obtain the salvation which is in Christ Jesus and with it eternal glory" (2 Timothy 2:10).

8. Trials will open up for you a new understanding of Scripture. The psalmist wrote, "It is good for me that I was afflicted, that I may learn Your statutes" (Psalm 119:71).

9. Trials will enhance your fellowship with Christ. Paul desired "the surpassing value of knowing Christ Jesus" and yearned to "know Him and the power of His resurrection and the *fellowship of His sufferings*, being conformed to His death" (Philippians 3:8, 10, italics added).

A Relationship with the Eternal God Gives Us a Sense of Anticipation

Though Western Christians are not subject yet to such persecution, we should ask ourselves how first-century believers "accepted joyfully the seizure of [their] property" (Hebrews 10:34) and the apostle Paul could regard the list of afflictions in 2 Corinthians 11:23–27 as "light" (2 Corinthians

4:17). The answer? It is only through the perspective of a relationship with our eternal God and what that relationship allows us to anticipate (2 Corinthians 4:18).

When you think of your future heavenly hope, does it get you excited? On the day of D. L. Moody's death, he seemed to catch a glimpse of heaven. He said, "This is my coronation day! I have been looking forward to this for years."[7]

Revelation 7:15–17 gives us a glimpse into a scene in heaven. What awaits includes *the enjoyment of His presence* ("He who sits on the throne will spread His tabernacle over them" [v. 15]); *perfect satisfaction* ("They will hunger no more, nor thirst anymore" [v. 16]); and *perfect comfort* ("nor will the sun beat down on them . . ." and "God will wipe every tear from their eyes. . ." [vv. 16, 17]). Finally, during eternity with God and His Son, we will experience *perfect companionship and perfect guidance* ("The Lamb in the center of the throne will be their shepherd, and will guide them to springs of the water of life" [v. 17]).

What do you anticipate experiencing for all eternity? When you have been hurt or misunderstood, the experience of comfort can be a great balm to the soul. Do you realize that God said His comfort and consolation will never come to an end but is said to be eternal (2 Thessalonians 2:16)? His Word also teaches us that a Christian's experience of joy will never end: "In Your right hand there are pleasures forever" (Psalm 16:11). If you have been wronged or falsely accused, you can rest in the truth that God will eternally vindicate you, for He says, "Truthful lips will be established forever, but a lying tongue is only for a moment" (Proverbs 12:19).

Is it any wonder that one thing that will characterize our lives for all eternity is praise of our eternal God, the one "blessed forever" (Romans 1:25)? He will never run out of fresh ways to bestow His love on His people for all eternity.

Notes

1. Richard Polle, *Christianity Today*, September 2006, 112.

2. Lawrence Scupoli, *Christianity Today*, September 2006, 112.

3. For this concept in relationship to waiting on God for a mate, see Bill Thrasher, *Believing God for His Best: How to Marry Contentment and Singleness* (Chicago: Moody, 2004).

4. Robert J. Morgan *On This Day: 365 Amazing and Inspiring Stories about Saints, Martyrs & Heroes* (Nashville: Nelson, 1997), July 16.

5. Randy Alcorn, *Heaven* (Carol Stream, Ill.: Tyndale, 2004), xxii.

6. For more detail on how trials can let you better know the God of all comfort, see Bill Thrasher, *How to Be a Soul Physician* (Seattle: CreateSpace, 2010), 172–76. The book can be found at the author's website, www.victoriouspraying.com.

7. Lyle Dorsett, *A Passion for Souls* (Chicago: Moody, 1997), 381.

Part Three

AN ALL-KNOWING, WISE, EVER-PRESENT, AND ALL-POWERFUL GOD

7

God Is Omniscient
HE KNOWS ALL THINGS

*G*OD KNOWS EVERYTHING. Nothing happens, has happened, nor will happen that He does not know. In a personal psalm, King David declared many truths about God's knowledge of our lives:

> O Lord, You have searched me and known me. You know when I sit down and when I rise up; You understand my thought from afar. You scrutinize my path and my lying down, and are intimately acquainted with all my ways. Even before there is a word on my tongue, behold, O Lord, You know it all. You have enclosed me behind and before, and laid Your hand upon me. Such knowledge is too wonderful for me; it is too high, I cannot attain to it. (Psalm 139:1–6)

God knows *all* things! He is never surprised or taken off guard by some new development. While He has chosen to reveal this "wonderful" truth (Psalm 139:6) in anthropomorphic or human terms such as "searching" (Psalm 139:1), He has eternally and perfectly known all things. His knowledge is instant and effortless as He alone does not have to learn or seek man's counsel in order to gain knowledge.

His questioning of man is not to gain information He does not know, but rather to get His finite creatures in touch with the reality of their omniscient Creator. For example, consider God's question, "Where are you?" (Genesis 3:9), and Jesus' question, "Where are we to buy bread, so that these may eat?" (John 6:5). God knew where Adam and Eve were in the garden of Eden. And John tells us Jesus asked the question "to test [Philip], for He Himself knew what He was intending to do" (6:6).

God Knows Himself

God alone is the only person who has perfect knowledge of Himself. There is no human who has perfect insight and knowledge of himself. Yet during the numerous times when in our weakness we do not know how to fully express what is on our hearts (Romans 8:26), we can still rest in the Father's perfect knowledge of the mind of the Spirit who prays our deep longings when we are unable to do so (Romans 8:27).[1]

We need to look to Him not only to aid us in expressing our own hearts but also to reveal Himself to us (Matthew 11:25–27).

He Knows Everything
About the Past, Present, and Future

God knows all about the past. The eternal God has witnessed it all. But beyond actions in the open, He knows about actions done in secret. He also knows people's thoughts. He knows all that you have ever thought, said, or done — and the thoughts, words, and actions of everyone else as well. Later we will talk about His judicial and gracious forgetfulness!

Today God remains fully aware of His inanimate creation, His animal creation, and His human creation. He knows the number of the stars that exist and has even given a name to each one (Psalm 147:4). There is no detail that He does not know, such as the number of snowflakes — which change from minute to minute — and the design and shape of each one.

He knows about and cares for all the creatures. Jesus tells us that not a sparrow falls to the ground apart from His intimate knowledge (Matthew 10:29). He even knows what every bird had for breakfast as well as every lion (Job 38:39–41)! He knows the birthday of every goat and deer (Job 39:1). God instructs Job, and it's clear that not even the slightest detail is outside of the knowledge of God.

God also knows about His human creation. The "eyes of the Lord are in every place" (Proverbs 15:3). He not only knows the number of hairs on every person's head (Matthew 10:30) but also knows the thoughts and intentions of every person (Psalm 139:1–6; Jeremiah 17:10).

God also knows the future. At various times God has announced through prophets future events, including the coming of His Son to earth. Prophecy is as natural to Him as history. Everything outside of Himself was once future from our perspective.

God knows what could happen, and what would happen if something else had happened (see 2 Kings 13:19; Matthew 11:21–23). He even knows all that you can even imagine (Ephesians 3:20)!

Standing in Awe of God's Omniscience

The whole spirit of Psalm 139 is one of awe! God's perfect knowledge sets Him apart from the most brilliant person or the most prestigious library in the entire world. As we relate to our all-knowing God, how can we ever be proud of our knowledge?

What would you do if someone came up to you while you were reading this book and they knew everything you had ever thought or imagined, every word you had ever uttered, and everything you had ever done? Most of us would have a profound sense of fear and shame. The truth is that a person is with you right now who meets the above description— He knows everything about you. Yet God, who knows our selfish thoughts and attitudes, offers forgiveness to us. He knew we would sin—transgress against His law—and yet He has provided for forgiveness and reconciliation with Him.

The Scripture declares, "God demonstrates His own love toward us, in that while we were yet sinners, Christ died for us" (Romans 5:8). He knew before we were born we would sin. The awesome truth is that He sacrificed His Son in order to allow you to be fully and completely forgiven and to enjoy His perfect love! When this hits your heart, you will never be the same again (Psalm 130:1–3).

There is someone who knows and perfectly understands you. He knows your needs, your desires, your trials, and your battles. He knows the solution of every problem you will ever have. When you lose something, is your first instinct to pray to the One who knows where it is? Often we are not drawing the comfort from God's omniscience that we can. Take comfort in this truth. The psalmist found such comfort, marveling that "such knowledge is too wonderful for me" (Psalm 139:6).

The Comfort of His Fellowship

The omnipotence of God offers other comforts to His followers as well. We have fellowship with One whose "understanding is infinite" (Psalm 147:5). He is able to perfectly understand you and me in our loneliness, heartaches, and misunderstandings, as well as our joys (Psalm 38:9). In fact He is always thinking about us. He never takes His mind off you and me! The psalmist declares, "How precious also are Your thoughts to me, O God! How vast is the sum of them! If I should count them, they would outnumber the sand" (Psalm 139:17–18).

As you fellowship with Him in prayer, rest in the truth that He knows all the needs of the world as well as your own, and depend on His leading as you pray — knowing that He is eager to guide you and to listen to you.[2]

The Comfort of His Guidance

Out of the deep riches of His knowledge, God is able to guide you because He does not have to depend on any other person to counsel Him (Romans 11:33–34). He is able to blend His perfect knowledge of you — your strengths, weaknesses, and gifts — with His perfect knowledge of every possibility and His perfect knowledge of every other person and all the needs of the world.

God was aware of His people's suffering in Egypt at the hands of their cruel taskmasters. Their cry for a deliverer was not falling on deaf ears (Exodus 3:7–9). God was at work humbling and training Moses in the wilderness for forty years after he had fled Egypt. In His perfect timing, He called Moses to be their deliverer.

You too probably will be the answer to someone's prayers as you heed God's call on your life. Perhaps there is a dear lady crying out to God for a husband or a man crying to God for a wife and you may be the answer. You could be the answer to someone's cries to send a laborer to some mission field at home or abroad. Whether your mission field is in your own family, the corporate world, your church, a mission organization, or wherever, the key is to always be open to the leading of your omniscient Shepherd who is willing to guide you in the paths of righteousness for His name's sake (Psalm 23:3). (For more on His guidance for our lives, see chapter 8 on the wisdom of God.)

The Comfort of His Instruction

One day as I was studying, the thought occurred to me that since God is omnipotent (all-powerful) and omniscient (all-knowing), He could just effortlessly put all these truths in my head. However, He has not chosen to do this but has rather initiated the learning process. It hit me that He desires me to look to Him to teach me. I need to depend on Him to teach me all that I need to know. In other words, if I am studying and learning as He desires, I am building a relationship with Him and also letting the truths I learn transform my life.

The omniscient God has given us a revelation of all the

truth we need. It is sufficient for salvation (2 Timothy 3:15; see also Luke 16:31) and also sufficient to equip God's people for "every good work" (2 Timothy 3:16–17). There are "secret things" that only God knows and has chosen not to reveal (Deuteronomy 29:29).

Christ called His disciples His friends, and after challenging them to obedience, He said that He will not withhold from them any knowledge that they will need to know (John 15:14–15). So it is with you and me. He gives us what we need to know but no more.

Before I entered my seminary training, I cried to God for Him to give me a detailed vision of my future ministry. The request was based on the idea that such knowledge could enrich and focus my years of preparation. While such a request is not wrong and God may indeed give you this, He never did answer this in my life. He has always given me the guidance I need and taught me to be content with my daily bread of guidance. He knew my having such knowledge of my future could have easily taken me away from the present. It also would have resulted in my focusing more on my future tasks than my present development. John Wesley once said, "Don't seek for a ministry, but anticipate the fruit of a disciplined life." God's withholding my request was His kind way of helping me to focus on the right thing.

The Comfort of His Reward and Vindication

A reporter for the *Washington Post* conducted an experiment to see if people would appreciate and recognize the skill of a renowned violinist if he were stationed in an ordinary setting. Joshua Bell, dressed in jeans, a T-shirt, and a Washington Nationals baseball hat, positioned himself by a trash basket beside the Metro during the morning commute. Thousands of people passed by the next forty-five minutes as he played his rare Stradivarius violin worth over three million dollars.

Bell played works by Mozart and Schubert on his instrument. But the world-renowned violinist was virtually unnoticed, collecting only thirty-two dollars from the twenty-seven commuters who stopped by long enough to give a donation. Three days earlier he had played to a sold-out Boston Symphony Hall.[3]

Most of God's magnificent work is done without fanfare or notice. Similarly, the sacrificial missionary, hardworking mother, faithful office worker, church nursery worker, and a host of other servants of God are largely unsung heroes.

Every human has a desire within to be noticed and to know that his or her efforts are pleasing and fruitful. Yet for those who minister for the honor of God, their desire changes; their comfort comes in knowing God witnesses all their actions. The apostle Paul found his comfort in knowing that God knew of the apostle's prayer life (Romans 1:9), his love for others (Philippians 1:8), and even the motives of his heart (1 Thessalonians 2:4–5, 10). This is a great comfort to the one who makes as his supreme goal to be pleasing to the One who knows all the facts (Galatians 1:10).

Admitting Our Sins

The prophet Isaiah speaks of those who try to hide their plans from the Lord and live under the illusion that no one sees or knows what they do in the dark (Isaiah 29:15). When you are entertaining these deceitful thoughts, remember these truths from God's Word.

The eyes of the Lord are in every place, watching the evil and the good. (Proverbs 15:3)

There is no creature hidden from His sight, but all things are open and laid bare to the eyes of Him with whom we have to do. (Hebrews 4:13)

There is nothing covered up that will not be revealed, and hidden that will not be known. Accordingly, whatever you have said in the dark will be heard in the light, and what you have whispered in the inner rooms will be proclaimed upon the housetops. (Luke 12:2–3)

In light of these truths, every "secret" sin is in reality an open scandal, for God knows every thought, word, and deed. We are to live as if always in public view — as if someone was always looking into our minds — for God does know our thoughts.

The Pathway to True Joy

There is no more fitting conclusion to our discussion of God's omniscience than the challenge to walk in the light (1 John 1:7). To walk in the light means to walk openly, honestly, and transparently before the Lord and His truth. It involves inviting the Lord to search our hearts to see if there is any area of our thinking or life that is not in harmony with God (Psalm 139:23). To "confess our sins" (1 John 1:9) means "to say the same thing" or agree with God as He points out sin in our life.

The result of such transparency before an all-knowing God is to enjoy God's continual cleansing that allows us to continue in fellowship with the Lord.[4] *This fellowship is the key to joy* (1 John 1:4). When you and God are in agreement, you can be joyful no matter what else may be happening. This is why Jesus, though a man of sorrows, was the most joyful person who ever lived (see Hebrews 1:9). He lived in perfect harmony with His righteous and omniscient Father as He walked this earth as the God-man. His life has set a pattern for us (1 John 2:6).

May you know the joy of walking with your omniscient Father God today.

Notes

1. For a greater explanation of this truth, see Bill Thrasher, *A Journey to Victorious Praying* (Chicago: Moody, 2003), 57–60.

2. For further instructions about how to follow the Spirit's leading in prayer, see Ibid., 51–56.

3. Gene Weingarten, "Pearls Before Breakfast," *Washington Post*, 10 April 2007.

4. For more insight in appropriating Christ's continual cleansing, see Bill Thrasher, *How to Be a Soul Physician* (Seattle: CreateSpace, 2010), 211–34. The book can be found at the author's website, www.victoriouspraying.com.

8

God Is Wise

HE DESIRES TO
SHARE HIS WISDOM

*G*OD HAS THE ABILITY to formulate the best plans and purposes and to achieve them by the best means. God knows all things, and His knowledge can be said to be the root of His wisdom, and His wisdom the flower of His knowledge. His wisdom is the use of His knowledge for its highest purpose.

The apostle Paul describes almighty God as "the only wise God" (Romans 16:27). The prophet Daniel, highlighting God's wisdom and power, blesses his Creator:

> Let the name of God be blessed forever and ever, for wisdom and power belong to Him. It is He who changes the times and the epochs; He removes kings and establishes kings; He gives wisdom to wise men and knowledge to men of understanding. It is He who reveals the

profound and hidden things; He knows what is in the darkness, and the light dwells with Him. To You, O God of my fathers, I give thanks and praise, for You have given me wisdom and power; even now You have made known to me what we requested of You, for You have made known to us the king's matter. (Daniel 2:20–23)

The Manifold,
Unsearchable Wisdom of God

As Paul presented the gospel to the Gentiles, he declared the riches of Christ and God's mystery. He now revealed what once had been hidden, "the manifold wisdom of God" (Ephesians 3:8–10). What did Paul mean when he called God's wisdom "manifold" (v. 10)?

Strands of truth, infinite diversity, and sparkling beauty characterize God's wisdom. With His wisdom God can work out solutions to hopeless and confusing problems. We never can understand the many elements of His wisdom, but like Daniel we can marvel at it and find rest that His wisdom can inform our lives.

Paul also describes the wisdom of God as unsearchable (see Romans 11:33). His wisdom is unsearchable in that no one can exhaustively comprehend it. Not only are there secrets that God has not revealed (Deuteronomy 29:29), but there is an unsearchable quality to even His revealed truth. For example, one can know the truth of the revelation of the Trinity and God's sovereign plan. However, the knowledge of these truths is only partial, and we bow in worship as we realize our limits and God's wisdom.

There is even an unsearchable nature to the workings of His providential wisdom in our own lives. As Solomon wrote,

"Man's steps are ordained by the Lord, how then can man understand his way?" (Proverbs 20:24).

His Wisdom Shown in His Creation — Including Us

God's wisdom in His creation is highlighted in the Wisdom Literature of the Bible (Job through Song of Solomon). Here are two examples:

O Lord, how many are Your works! In wisdom You have made them all; the earth is full of Your possessions. (Psalm 104:24)

The Lord by wisdom founded the earth, by understanding He established the heavens. (Proverbs 3:19)

God's creative design is full of variety, beauty, and order, and shows His merciful provisions for His creation. The question for us is, do we accept His wise design of our life? If I were to offer you a magic wand that you could use to change any unchangeable feature of your life — such as your heritage, your gender, your parents — would you use it? Many times a day we have thoughts that go through our mind that make us desire this magic wand.

Are you willing to let your wise Father teach you that His will is exactly what you would desire if you knew all the facts? He is a wise Creator and He wants you to know that you are "fearfully and wonderfully made" and for your soul to know this truth very well (Psalm 139:14).[1]

His Wisdom
Revealed in Christ

In Christ are "hidden all the treasures of wisdom and knowledge" (Colossians 2:3). In Him God's wise plan of salvation was realized. God in His wisdom overrules evil — even the greatest act of terrorism ever performed — to bring about the greatest blessing the world has ever known. As Peter put it: "This Man, delivered over by the predetermined plan and foreknowledge of God, you nailed to a cross by the hands of godless men and put Him to death" (Acts 2:23).

In Christ God displayed His love, grace, and mercy as well as His righteousness and wrath at the same time (Romans 3:24–26). For this reason we can boast in His greatest accomplishment on the cross of Christ (Galatians 6:14).

Christ also displayed wisdom in His earthly life as He demonstrated how God intended man to live (1 John 2:6). He gave us the pattern of what it means to be successful (John 17:4)!

God's Wisdom Shown
in His Sovereign Plan

God's wisdom guides His providential dealings in which He works "all things after the counsel of His will" (Ephesians 1:11). In His wisdom He rules and overrules everything — even the smallest details — for the ultimate good of His people. Thus Paul declares, under the Spirit's illumination, "We know that God causes all things to work together for good to those who love God, to those who are called according to His purpose" (Romans 8:28).

In His wisdom, His eternal plan (1 Peter 1:20) is executed in perfect timing (Galatians 4:4; Romans 5:6).

In God's wise, sovereign plan, He uses not only a great diversity of gifts and people (1 Corinthians 12:22–26) but also the weak and foolish things of the world in order to display His wisdom (1 Corinthians 1:26–31; 2 Corinthians 12:9–10). God's wise plan excludes improper human boasting (1 Corinthians 1:29) and results in the "praise of His glory" (Ephesians 1:12, 14) and all things being subjected to Him (Ephesians 1:22).

We should understand that His glory — the display of His attributes — is so unlike man trying to get glory. Out of the need of our hearts, we can try to get glory at others' expense to make ourselves look good. God — who is in need of nothing — gets His glory by coming to earth as a baby, being born in poverty, and dying for His enemies! How grateful we are for a wise, sovereign plan that begins and ends with His glory!

In His goodness God desires your highest welfare. God in His power is able to bring this about. In His wisdom God has planned all of this for you. All of our boasting is to be in our weakness (2 Corinthians 12:9) and His greatness (1 Corinthians 1:31).

God Offers His Wisdom

Wisdom is personified in Proverbs and cries out and invites people to learn (see, for example, 1:20–23; 8:1–36; 9:1–6). The sad commentary of these passages is that few people take advantage of wisdom's invitation. This is why we find large parts of our sociological structures in our society void of God's wisdom.

Yet God offers us His wisdom. If you were to come to God and ask Him for wisdom, what exactly would you get? This gift is so wonderful that it is difficult to sum it up in a single definition. Let me offer you three.

First, wisdom is the ability to see life from God's point of view. From God's point of view, we have learned that this Christ is not only the wisdom of God (1 Corinthians 1:24) but also our very life (Philippians 1:21; Colossians 3:4).

When you are burdened down and irritated about a certain trial, you can cry to God for wisdom (James 1:5). I have found it helpful to ask others as well to intercede for me that I may know how to view this trial from God's perspective. There have been times that the burden has become lighter even without God changing the circumstances because of the different perspective that He has given. He may even be pleased to share with you the good that He is working out of your present difficulty (see Genesis 50:20).

Second, wisdom is the ability to select the best goals for one's life and the best means to fulfill them. The year that I was set to complete my doctoral studies, I felt compelled to pray in this way: "Lord, help me to aim my life at the right thing." I had a fear of aiming my life at the wrong thing, achieving it, and at the end of my life discovering that the ladder I had climbed was leaning against the wrong wall. My prayer was, "Lord, help me to aim my life at that which is at the center of Your heart."

That prayer is a prayer for wisdom. I believe that a significant part of the answer of that prayer was God directing me to focus on His attributes in my life and ministry.

What are His goals for you? God knows. Through prayer and Scripture seek to learn His goals for you.

Third, wisdom is the ability to live with skill before God. There are skills that can make one useful, such as the skill of carpentry. The skilled craftsmen who built the tabernacle were endowed with wisdom (Exodus 31:3). There is also a skill of living life. Proverbs is designed to train one in these skills. For example, there is a skill in using your tongue, in handling your money, and in relating to people. Our wise God yearns to share with us the skill we all desperately need in our relationships, marriages, families, and churches.

His Guidance

We struggle in all three of these areas of wisdom, but most of us struggle to determine the best goals for our life. We want wisdom to know what to do. Yet often we choose to figure out things for ourselves.

Always be open to the leading of the Father, who is willing to guide you in the paths of righteousness for His name's sake (Psalm 23:3). Look to Him even when you *think* you know what path to take. Read the story of how God's people were deceived by the Gibeonites because they "did not ask for the counsel of the Lord" (Joshua 9:14).

There was a time in my singleness that I had a strong desire to initiate a friendship with a certain young woman, but I sensed a strong prompting to not do so. I argued with the Lord about this. During this time, I visited a church with a group of friends. In his message that morning, the pastor told how the elders and he concluded that a certain man outside of their fellowship would be a perfect person to be invited to join the staff of their church. The pastor agreed to have lunch with this man to talk about the position. When the two met, the pastor felt no peace about bringing up this topic. In fact the lunch ended with no discussion of this issue. He later reported apologetically to the elders about the meeting. A short time later something was exposed in this "potential" new staff member's life, and the elder board worshiped God for not allowing this to blow up in the midst of their fellowship.

Sometimes we may think we know what is best but always look to God's counsel to confirm. I have made it a policy to never make a key decision on the spot. It is seldom necessary to do so, and after sleeping on it for a while, you usually can see certain implications that may not have occurred to you earlier.

I never had the freedom to pursue a relationship with that fine young lady. I do not think anything was wrong with her, but I do know that God had more single years in preparing me for the wonderful girl He had for me later.

We can trust the wise God to not only provide for us but even to prepare us for what is ahead. Sometimes the way He prepares us is to not let us know too far in advance.[2]

The Value of Wisdom

If I had two packages to offer you, and you were to choose only one of them, which would you choose: One that contains the gift of wisdom, or one that contains all the things you desire?

You may be familiar with the proverb, "Wisdom is better than jewels; and all desirable things cannot compare with her" (Proverbs 8:11). One summer as I pondered this verse, I humbly told God that my emotions did not believe this truth. On my heart at that time was a young lady whom I deeply desired. She was a "desirable thing." I told the Lord that I believed Proverbs 8:11 was true and wanted that belief to even refocus my emotions. My plan was that every time I felt a desire for this young lady, I would pray that God would teach my heart the value of wisdom. You could have all the things you desire, but without God's wisdom you would not even know how to truly enjoy them. (I should add that eventually this woman would become my wife — though at that point I was not on her heart at all!)

Avoid the Counterfeit Wisdom

When God has a valuable gift to give, this world will offer a substitute. Jesus alluded to this when He explained that the peace He offered was unlike the counterfeit peace the world offered. "Peace I leave with you," He said; "My peace I give to you; not as the world gives do I give to you. Do not let your heart be troubled, nor let it be fearful" (John 14:27).

Similarly, there is a wisdom that does not come "from above, but is earthly, natural, and demonic," the Scripture declares (James 3:15). The chart on the following page reveals some of the contrasts between the wisdom of the world and the wisdom of God.

You will notice that the motivating force of the world's wisdom is selfish ambition. There is nothing wrong with ambition as long as it is under the control of God. Apart from Jesus' liberating death and the enablement of His Spirit, we are all sentenced to live under the motivation of our selfish ambition. We will examine next the devastating results of living by this wisdom.

Results of Living by
the Wisdom of the World

After you review the chart "Counterfeit Versus Real Wisdom," ask God to show you what areas of your life are

Table 3
Counterfeit Versus Real Wisdom

Wisdom of the World	Wisdom of God
Rejects God's revelation (Romans 1:22).	Submits mind to Scripture (Psalm 119:27).
Product of human thinking alone (Proverbs 14:12).	Submits mind to the teaching of the Spirit (1 Corinthians 2:11–13).
Misunderstands or ignores Christ and the cross (1 Corinthians 1:18; 2:8).	Adores and boasts in Christ and His cross (1 Corinthians 1:24, 30; Galatians 6:14).
Boasts in man and what he can do (1 Corinthians 3:4, 21).	Boasts in God and His grace (1 Corinthians 1:30; 15:6–10).
Motivated by selfish ambition (James 3:14–15).	Motivated by the Holy Spirit for God's glory (Psalm 115:1; John 16:14).

being directed and influenced by the wisdom of the world. This is not only a theoretical issue, because there are concrete consequences of being influenced by ideas that do not come from our wise God.

What are these devastating results? When our lives are ruled by the selfish ambition that is the motivating force of the world's wisdom, the results are "disorder and every evil thing" (James 3:16). The disorder is not only in our outward world but also an internal disorder or restless spirit. The verse describes a life out of fellowship with the God who is characterized by order and peace (1 Corinthians 14:33). The Greek word for "evil" in James 3:16 speaks of that which is "good for nothing" or vain. No true gain comes from living independent of God. The wisdom of the world is not consistent with abiding in the Lord (John 15:5) and learning to labor in His strength (Colossians 1:29).

Such disorder leads to a life of vanity. The psalmist tells us, "Unless the Lord builds the house, they labor in vain who build it; unless the Lord guards the city, the watchman keeps awake in vain. It is vain for you to rise up early, to retire late, to eat the bread of painful labors; for He gives to His beloved even in his sleep" (Psalm 127:1–2).

Discerning God's Wisdom

No one wants to live a life of "disorder" and vanity. How can we discern God's wisdom? Besides recognizing the counterfeit wisdom shown in table 3, we can expect God's wisdom to always be in harmony with three things: the principles of God's Word, the Scriptures; the character of Christ; and the qualities mentioned in James 3:17–18 — being pure, peaceable, gentle, reasonable, full of mercy, unwavering, and without hypocrisy. Let's consider all three.

First, God's wisdom will always be in harmony with the principles of His Word. God told His people Israel that if they obeyed the principles of His Word, other nations would respond by saying, "Surely this great nation is a wise and understanding people" (Deuteronomy 4:6).

Yet God's principles are often contrary to our natural inclinations. J. B. Phillips noted how our Lord's beatitudes are quite different from the messages we often get in the world. For example, look at these contrasts:

- Happy are the pushers, for they get on in the world.
- Jesus said happy are those who realize their spiritual poverty.

- Happy are those who protect themselves from the pain of caring for others, for they will never let life hurt them.
- Jesus said happy are those who mourn.

- Happy are those who complain, for they get their way in the end.
- Jesus said happy are those who accept life and their own limitations and show gentleness to others.[3]

During the twentieth century, Presidents Dwight Eisenhower, Ronald Reagan, and Bill Clinton variously attributed the following statement to "a wise philosopher [who] came to this country" and to historian Alexis de Tocqueville in his classic study *Democracy in America*.[4]

I sought for the greatness and genius of America in her commodious harbors and her ample rivers—and it was not there. . . . I sought for it in her rich mines, her vast world commerce, her public schools system, and in her institutions of higher learning—and it was not there. . . . I looked for it in her democratic Congress and her matchless constitution—and it was not there. Not until I went into the churches of America and heard her pulpits flame with righteousness did I understand the secret of her genius and power. America is great because America is good, and if America ever ceases to be good, America will cease to be great![5]

God prospered our young nation, which had as its foundation many of the principles of God's Word. May God turn us back to Him and His Word, for only then can we truly become wise.

Second, God's wisdom will always be in harmony with the character of Christ. In Christ are "all the treasures of wisdom and knowledge" (Colossians 2:3). He is not only the source of all true wisdom but He also displayed this wisdom in His earthly life. His wise life reveals how to experience peace amidst great pressure (John 14:27), joy in the midst of great hardship (John 15:11), and success in the midst of great opposition (John 17:4). He is the revelation of how to live a wise life. The apostle John says we are to imitate Christ: "The one who says he abides in Him ought himself to walk in the same manner as He walked" (1 John 2:6).

Third, God's wisdom will always be in harmony with the qualities of James 3:17–18. One day as I was walking up to school from the train, I was writing a letter in my mind. It was one of those "touchy" letters that need to be written in order to deal with a misunderstanding and disagreement. By the time I got to school, I had the letter written in my mind. Fortunately that day I was teaching James 3. As I reviewed my lecture notes on James 3:17–18, I saw how wrong that letter was.

I thought I had been guided by God's wisdom, but I clearly had not been. My letter was not in harmony with these qualities found in James 3:17–18:

- *Pure.* Wise actions are free from the corruption of jealously and selfish ambition and in harmony with the purity of Christ (1 John 3:3).
- *Peaceable.* Wise actions will promote a right relationship between people but not at the expense of purity. However, even in disagreements, true wisdom hungers for peace (Romans 12:18).

- *Gentle.* Wise actions are considerate and respectful of the feelings of others.
- *Reasonable.* In our decisions we are teachable and submissive — the very opposite of being stubborn and unyielding.
- *Full of mercy and good fruits.* In our actions we display an attitude of compassion and deal with others in terms of what they need rather than what they deserve.
- *Unwavering.* Wise actions demonstrate consistency and impartiality.
- *Without hypocrisy.* Wise actions are sincere and genuine.

These truths enabled me to write a more appropriate letter that was guided by God's wisdom. These truths should guide us into wise, Christ-honoring decisions.

Seeking His Wisdom

I urge you to worship God as the only wise God. Trust His wisdom in both His creative design of you and the outworking of His sovereign plan in your life. If you do, you can pray with confidence for wisdom. See "Knowing Him" below for what to include in your prayers for wisdom.

Knowing Him

Praying for Wisdom

We can pray for God's wisdom for our decisions; that is part of the outworking of His sovereign plan in our lives. Here are elements to include in your prayers for wisdom:

1. Thank Him for the wisdom that He desires to share with you to enable you to view life from His point of view, to give you the right goals for your life and the right means to achieve them, and to enable you to live your life with skill.
2. Ask Him to show you that His wisdom is more valuable than all desirable things (Proverbs 8:11).
3. Ask God to show you how to distinguish between the wisdom of the world and His wisdom. As you do so, be alert to any input that promotes doubt in God's Word; any input that promotes putting your ultimate trust in man; and any input that promotes living independent of God.

As you await God's answer to your prayers, realize that God's wisdom may be contrary to your natural inclinations as you learn His ways and His thoughts, which are different from your ways and your thoughts. Observe the following paradoxes:

- The way to be first is to be last (Matthew 20:16).
- The way to gain is to lose (Philippians 3:8).
- The way to live and bear fruit is to die (John 12:24).
- The way to love is to hate (Luke 14:26).
- The way to get is to give (Luke 6:38).
- The way to resist is to surrender (Luke 6:29–30).
- The way to experience forgiveness is to forgive (Matthew 6:14–15).

Above all, purpose to seek His wisdom. Here are ten ways you can do that:

1. Recognize your need for wisdom. This requires being humble (Proverbs 11:2) and not being wise in your own eyes (Proverbs 3:7–8) but admitting that you are foolish (1 Corinthians 3:18) and unable to direct your path apart from His aid (Jeremiah 10:21). The Scripture says those who think they are wise in their own eyes become fools (Romans 1:22).
2. Recognize the value of wisdom and desire it above all else. Choosing wisdom above every other desirable thing is the right choice (1 Kings 3; 2 Chronicles 1:7–12; Proverbs 3:15; 8:11).
3. Cultivate a fear of God because the fear of God is the foundational principle of wisdom (Proverbs 9:10).
4. Diligently pursue the study of Scripture, because as you obey the Bible's commands, they will show you the path of wisdom (Deuteronomy 4:5–6; 2 Timothy 3:15).
5. Ask God for His wisdom, because He promises to give it generously (James 1:5).
6. Fellowship with wise people, because "he who walks with wise men will be wise" (Proverbs 13:20).
7. Maintain a teachable spirit and be willing to accept rebuke (Proverbs 9:8–9; 12:15; 21:11).
8. Flee evil because God says to "be wise in what is good but innocent in what is evil" (Romans 16:19).
9. Trust in God and not yourself, for "he who trusts in his own heart is a fool" (Proverbs 28:26).
10. Let your pursuit of wisdom be a great joy to you (Proverbs 10:23).

Worship, trust, and enjoy our wise God as you invite Him to share His wisdom with you.

Notes

1. For insights on having a right view of oneself, see Bill Thrasher, *Living the Life God Has Planned* (Chicago: Moody, 2001), 69–72.

2. For more insights into God's guidance, see *Living the Life God Has Planned: A Guide to Knowing God's Will* (Chicago: Moody, 2001). In the area of waiting on God for a spouse, see *Believing God for His Best: How to Marry Singleness and Contentment* (Chicago: Moody, 2004). Both books are written by the author.

3. J. B. Phillips, "The Beatitudes That Are," in Calvin Miller, ed., *The Book of Jesus* (New York: Simon & Schuster, 1998), 274.

4. Although typically attributed to Tocqueville, the quotation has never been located in *Democracy in America*. For an interesting search for the origin of the quotation, see John J. Pitney Jr., "The Tocqueville Fraud," *The Weekly Standard*, November 13, 1995, as cited at www.tocqueville.org.

5. Ibid., and in Grant Jeffrey, *The Signature of God* (New York: Inspirational Press, 1999), 25–26.

9

God Is Omnipresent

HE IS EVERYWHERE—
HE IS HERE

$\mathcal{H}$AVE YOU HEARD the poem about the neighbor who stopped the boy who had just walked back from Sunday school? Entitled "Where God Ain't," the poem's last two stanzas go like this:

> "M'm, very fine way," the neighbor said,
> "for a boy to spend his time"
> "If you'll tell me where God is,
> I'll give you a brand new dime."
>
> Quick as a flash the answer came,
> nor were his words faint
> "I'll give you a dollar, Mister,
> If you can tell me where God ain't."
>   Author Unknown[1]

The Bible tells us that God is present everywhere, but not everywhere in the same way. In fact, God's Word speaks of His presence in at least four ways: God is present (1) everywhere; (2) in His people; (3) in heaven; and (4) in our awareness of Him.

God Is Everywhere

King David seemed in awe of his always-present God as he wrote these verses in Psalm 139:

Where can I go from Your Spirit? Or where can I flee from Your presence? If I ascend to heaven, You are there; if I make my bed in Sheol, behold, You are there. If I take the wings of the dawn, if I dwell in the remotest part of the sea, even there Your hand will lead me, and Your right hand will lay hold of me. If I say, "Surely the darkness will overwhelm me, and the light around me will be night," even the darkness is not dark to You, and the night is as bright as the day. Darkness and light are alike to You. (vv. 7–12)

Speaking one day to a group of unbelievers, the apostle Paul said that God "is not far from each one of us, for in Him we live and move and exist" (Acts 17:27–28). In what way was Paul speaking of His presence? Was he speaking only of God's influential presence that exists throughout the world? There is the presence of His knowledge in that all things are laid bare before Him. There is the presence of His power as all things are sustained by Him. There is the presence of His authority as all things are subject to Him.

However, the attribute of omnipresence as presented in

Psalm 139:7–12 (and in Jeremiah 23:23–24 and Acts 17:27–28 as well) speaks of the *actual* presence of God's invisible essence that exists in all places and with all His creatures. What would it be like to continually be in the presence of One in whom you are not in harmony and not on speaking terms? Quite unpleasant!

To say that God is present everywhere in the world does not in any way mean that He is confined to this world and not present beyond it. Solomon exclaimed after the building of the temple, "Behold heaven and the highest heaven cannot contain You, how much less this house which I have built!" (1 Kings 8:27). Saying "God is present everywhere" does mean, however, that everywhere you go you can confidently say, "God is here."

God Is in His People

While the Scriptures teach that God is everywhere, they also affirm special manifestations of God's presence in the tabernacle (Exodus 40:34) and in the temple (1 Kings 8:12–13). In the present day, God's people are declared to be the temple of God because He indwells them. So God also is in His people.

Do you not know that your body is a temple of the Holy Spirit who is in you, whom you have from God, and that you are not your own? (1 Corinthians 6:19)

In whom the whole building, being fitted together, is growing into a holy temple in the Lord, in whom you also are being built together into a dwelling of God in the Spirit. (Ephesians 2:21–22)

God Is in Heaven

While Paul declared that even unbelievers live in God's presence (Acts 17:27–28), and believers are indwelt by God (1 Corinthians 6:19), he also anticipated the enjoyment of God's presence in heaven. He anticipated one day being absent or free from the limitations of his unredeemed body and this unredeemed world. In fact the apostle described his present state as being "absent from the Lord" (2 Corinthians 5:6) and his future in heaven as being "at home with the Lord" (2 Corinthians 5:8). Jesus taught His disciples to pray by first acknowledging their Father whose presence is in heaven (Matthew 6:9).

God Is Present in Our Awareness: Consciously Enjoying His Presence

Each semester on the first day of class, I pass out 3x5 cards to each student to write out a prayer request that they desire me to remember before the Lord. One year this was one student's request: "Lord, I want to know You in such a way that I miss You when I am not conscious of You."

I have heard people get rebuked on several occasions for such a request and then given a brief lecture on the omnipresence of God. However, the apostle Paul prayed, "Now the God of peace be with you all. Amen" (Romans 15:33). It is an appropriate prayer. For while it is true that God is everywhere and all believers, since the day of Pentecost, have had the permanent indwelling of the Holy Spirit (Romans 8:9), all believers do not always enjoy the presence of an ungrieved and unquenched Spirit. It is this kind of presence that accompanies the believer who continually trusts and obeys God

(Philippians 4:7). It is this kind of presence that caused an unbeliever to exclaim to Abraham, "God is with you in all that you do" (Genesis 21:22).[2]

So to the question "Is it correct to pray that God be with someone?" I answer, "Yes!"

In his classic book *The Practice of the Presence of God*, Brother Lawrence expressed his desire to be as aware of God's presence when he was washing the dishes as when he was having his devotions. According to A. W. Tozer, "We are saved to know God, to enter His wonder-filled presence through a new and living way and remain in that presence forever. We are called to an everlasting preoccupation with God" (*The Incredible Christian*). When we invite God into our daily lives, we can consciously enjoy His presence.

King David understood the importance of this truth, writing in Psalm 16:8, "I have set the Lord continually before me; because He is at my right hand, I will not be shaken."

Thus God's Word speaks of His presence in these four ways: God is everywhere; in His people; in heaven; and in our awareness, so we can consciously enjoy His presence.

The Goodness of God's Presence

One day I spoke to a crowd of well over one thousand students on the concept of practicing God's presence. One honest listener came up and expressed his reluctance to take on the challenge. He said, "I am not sure I want to bring the Lord into all of my activities." In his mind the Lord's presence might disrupt some of his joys.

That conversation caused me to look further at the way God describes His presence. Is His presence always good? Here's what the Scriptures say:

- God's presence is the place of *success* and *enablement* (Genesis 39:1–3, 21–23).
- God's presence is what *favors* and sets God's people apart from all other people (Exodus 33:16).
- God's presence is the place of *blessing* (2 Samuel 6:11).
- God's presence is the place of *stability* and *joy* (Psalm 16:8–9).
- God's presence is the place of *divine help* (Psalm 42:5).
- God's presence is the place of *satisfaction* (Psalm 65:4).
- God's presence is the place of *insight* and *perspective* (Psalm 73:17).
- God's presence is the place of *strength* and *beauty* (Psalm 96:6).
- God's presence is the place of *refreshment* (Acts 3:19).

God makes it look so attractive that it would be insane not to want to enjoy it.[3]

The Results of Having a Conscious Enjoyment of God's Presence

Suppose you invite your best friend to spend the day with you, and he anticipates this special day for many months. When the day finally arrives, he joins you for every second of that day. How would he feel if you never even acknowledged his presence? Of course, he would feel very slighted, and such rudeness seems almost unthinkable when you consider you are with your best friend.

Have we not been guilty of ignoring the presence of the One who is better than the best of men? Why not decide to honor and enjoy Him in all your activities of this day? When you do, you can anticipate these four outcomes.

Result 1: The Comfort of Knowing You Are Never Alone

Jesus bore the curse of our sins in order to allow us to experience the blessings of God's presence (Galatians 3:13–14). One of these curses was the curse of being forsaken by a holy God whose eyes are too pure to behold evil (Habakkuk 1:13). Jesus bore this curse while hanging on the cross. The Scripture says: "About the ninth hour Jesus cried out with a loud voice, saying, 'Eli, Eli, Lama Sabachthani?' that is, 'My God, my God, why have You forsaken Me?'" (Matthew 27:46).

In enduring this isolation, Jesus Christ earned for us the blessing of fellowship with God our Father: Make sure that your character is free from the love of money, being content with what you have; for He Himself has said, 'I will never desert you, nor will I ever forsake you'" (Hebrews 13:5).

If you have acknowledged your sins and looked to Christ alone for your salvation, you have been given the gracious promise that you will never, ever have to be alone. You may be suffering and feel misunderstood, but you can know the comfort of not being alone. You may be a widow, a widower, a single parent, or even abandoned, but you are not alone if you are a Christian.

The apostle Paul in the last days of hs life knew what it was like to be supported by no one and deserted by everyone! He also knew what it was like to experience the Lord's grace to forgive these deserters, and His presence and strength to accomplish God's purpose in the midst of it:

At my first defense no one supported me, but all deserted me; may it not be counted against them. But the Lord stood with me and strengthened me, so that through me the proclamation might be fully accomplished, and that all the Gentiles might hear; and I was rescued out of the lion's mouth. (2 Timothy 4:16–17)

In any trial, temptation, or responsibility, you can count on the words of our Lord, "Lo, I am with you always, even to the end of the age" (Matthew 28:20).

When David Livingstone, who had been a missionary in Africa, received an honorary degree from Glasgow University, he rose to speak. He looked quite gaunt. His left arm, which had been crushed by a lion, hung helplessly by his side. He announced his resolve to return to Africa without any hesitation and with great joy. As he spoke he stated, "Would you like me to tell you what supported me through the years of exile among a people whose language I could not understand and whose attitude toward me was always uncertain and often hostile? It was this, 'Lo, I am with you always, even to the end of the age!' On these words I staked everything. They never failed."[4]

Martin Luther, the German reformer, was asked one day, "Where would you be if all of your followers were to leave you?" He replied, "I will be right in the very hands of God."

Dallas Willard tells of a boy who, like him, had lost his mother as a young child. Lonely and sad, the boy would enter his father's room at night to ask permission to sleep with him. When he was assured that he was with his father and that his father's face was turned in his direction, only then could he sleep.

You can endure anything when you realize who it is that is with you—a perfect father, a perfect lover, a perfect friend, and a perfect protector. As a fish was created to live in the water and a bird to fly in the sky, so you were created to practice the presence of God. Perfect love, power, and wisdom are not any distance from you! Remember that the Lord is *your* refuge and strength, "a very present help in trouble" (Psalm 46:1). May you know this comfort today.

Result 2: Being Confident of His Presence When You're with Others

While we can be insensitive to the presence of other people, we can also be oversensitive to them. In other words, we can begin to live before them rather than before God. Prior to Timothy's visit to Corinth, God went before him through the words of Paul,

> If Timothy comes, see that he is with you without cause to be afraid, for he is doing the Lord's work, as I also am. So let no one despise him. But send him on his way in peace, so that he may come to me; for I expect him with the brethren. (1 Corinthians 16:10–11)

The Greek preposition translated "with" in 1 Corinthians 16:10 has been called the "face-to-face preposition." In other words, the idea is that timid Timothy was to be able to look anyone confidently in the eye — face-to-face — without cause to be afraid. I have prayed many times for God to go before me and others as I anticipated facing intimidating situations and have experienced His faithfulness. The key is to set the Lord before you (Psalm 16:8).

Count on His promised presence to aid you in the fear of man. Rely on the promise of Hebrews 13:5–6: "He Himself has said, 'I will never desert you, nor will I ever forsake you.' So that we confidently say, 'The Lord is my helper, I will not be afraid. What will man do to me?'" (Hebrews 13:5–6). Recall also the confident words of David, who, knowing God was the light of his life, could write, "Though a host encamp against me, my heart will not fear; though war arise against me, in spite of this I shall be confident" (Psalm 27:3). His confidence came from the hope he could "dwell in the house of the Lord all the days of my life, to behold the beauty of the Lord and to meditate in His temple" (Psalm 27:4).

Result 3: Experiencing the Purifying, Cleansing Effect of His Presence

The test of a person's character is what would one do if he or she knew nobody would find out. An employee probably would not steal right in front of an employer. It's incredible to think a person would commit adultery while their spouse could observe them. Yet all of our "private" actions are done in the very presence of God. God asked Israel rhetorically whether they could hide from His presence any more than Adam could:

> "Can a man hide himself in hiding places so I do not see him?" declares the Lord. "Do I not fill the heavens and the earth?" declares the Lord. (Jeremiah 23:24)

Of course we cannot hide our actions from Him. All our "secret sins" are really open scandals (see Psalm 90:8). We are to think, speak, and act and live in God's presence. Hebrews puts it this way: "No creature [is] hidden from His sight, but all things are open and laid bare to the eyes of Him with whom we have to do" (Hebrews 4:13).

As you read Paul's writings, look for these phrases: "in

the sight of God" (2 Corinthians 2:17; 4:2; 7:12; 8:21; 12:19) and "God is my witness" (Romans 1:9; 2 Corinthians 1:23; Philippians 1:8; 1 Thessalonians 2:5, 10). Paul lived in the purifying presence of God.

Result 4: The Contentment of His Presence

Contentment is realizing the sufficiency and ability of the Lord to provide everything we will ever need at any given moment in our life. It is therefore based on the fact of His promised presence (Hebrews 13:5). It is for this reason that the Scriptures speak of being satisfied in God's presence (Psalm 65:4).

When we cultivate God's presence in our lives, there are many positive outcomes. Conversely, when we ignore or grieve God's presence, there are many negative consequences, as noted in table 4 on the following page.

The Greatest Compliment One Could Give a Church

Would you pray that God would open your eyes to see the reality of Christ's presence with you? Would you pray that God would so manifest Himself to you and your church that even an unbeliever could acknowledge the reality of Christ in your midst? There is no greater compliment a believer can give a church after departing it than to say, "God is in that place."

"God's presence must abide so heavily in our churches that they are distinctive from every other competitor in the

Table 4
Consequences of Cultivating—
Or Ignoring—God's Presence

When We Cultivate and Enjoy God's Presence	When We Ignore, Grieve, and Quench God's Presence
We honor God	We dishonor God
We are comforted	We are troubled
We are confident	We are fearful
We feel clean	We are impure and dirty
We are content	We are unfulfilled

religious supermarket. God's presence must dwell so pow-
erfully in our churches that even people who don't believe
in words anymore are overcome by the living Word," writes
Robert Bakke. "God's presence must rest so tangibly on our
churches that the refugees from the post-modern battlefield
will sense Him even when they don't have a category to
understand Him."[5]

Such manifestations in our churches have resulted in
past revivals. Those revivals led to an intense hunger to know
Jesus (Philippians 3:10); lives of joy, prayer, and thanksgiving (1 Thessalonians 5:16–18); decisive breaks with sin (Titus
2:12; Proverbs 28:13); and an overflowing love for others that
has transformed individuals, families, churches, and com-
munities. Such transformations involved parents finding joy
in their children as if they had just been born and husbands
and wives rejoicing over each other. There was a new eager-
ness to listen to God's Word, and the glories of Christ were
what began to dominate even ordinary social conversations.
As you respond to the last part of this chapter, may it be

used to spark a personal revival in your life and in the lives of others.

Enjoying the Presence of God

The Scriptures point to five ways we can experience God's presence in our lives. These five, which are detailed in the section "How to Cultivate a Conscious Enjoyment of God's Presence," are:

1. Ask God to show you any rebellion or double-mindedness (James 4:7–8).
2. Repent of sinful thoughts and actions (James 4:9–10).
3. Continually deal with any disagreement with God. Confess your sins regularly; they break your fellowship with God (1 John 1:7).
4. Learn to delight in God's presence (Psalm 37:4).
5. Be alert to reminders of His presence. Both blessings and trials are legitimate reminders of His presence and care for you (James 1:17; Romans 8:28, 35–37).

How to Cultivate a
Conscious Enjoyment of God's Presence

Knowing the many benefits of cultivating God's presence (review table 4), you may wonder, *How can I cultivate a conscious enjoyment of God's presence?* We conclude this chapter with five ways to cultivate God's presence in our lives.

First, ask God to show you any rebellion or double-mindedness in your life.

The command to "draw near to God" is followed up by the command to "purify your hearts, you double-minded" (James 4:8). Both follow the command to "submit . . . to God" (James 4:7). We need to first submit to His authority over us before we will be conscious of His presence with us! If we rebel, His presence cannot abide with us.

We must be careful to avoid the condition of being double-minded. "Double-mindedness" is the condition of trying to live for God *and* something else. One who is double-minded has a greater loyalty to some desire or drive in their life than their desire to obey God. Let's look at some signposts and the cure of this condition.

Ask God to search your heart as you consider these five signs of being double-minded, without a single focus on honoring God:

1. *A desire to be popular.* Are you willing to obey God even if it were to cost you your popularity or favor with someone in your life?
2. *A desire to be your own boss.* Are you consciously or unconsciously driven by desire to not let anyone else tell you what to do? Has some past hurt by an authority fueled this drive?
3. *A desire to get revenge.* Are you willing to yield to God your desire to prove yourself to be right? When you are wronged do you have a subtle drive to take your own revenge?
4. *A desire to be rich.* Is your desire to get rich greater than your desire to obey God? Are you willing to make little compromises in order to promote your financial gain?
5. *A desire to be lustful.* Is fulfilling any of your sensual lusts outside of God's will an option for you? Are you

as sensitive to sin in your life as the pupil of your eye is to foreign matter?

Second, repent of any double-minded thoughts and actions. When we recognize our double-mindedness, we should respond to God's gracious conviction. He has helped us realize we are not truly living for God. Respond to God's gracious enablement to repent by acknowledging your wrong god and placing yourself under God's loving authority.

There is a healthy form of repentance that can lead to regret and even tears. As James wrote, "Be miserable and mourn and weep; let your laughter be turned into mourning and your joy to gloom" (James 4:9).

God will welcome you and cleanse you as you draw near to Him (James 4:8). He can even exalt you for His purposes as you humble yourself before Him (v. 10).

When you repent, God gives you a pure heart. A pure heart is a united heart, one in which a man or woman is united with God, not broken from fellowship due to sin. You can follow the psalmist in praying this prayer: "Unite my heart to fear Your name" (Psalm 86:11).

Look at the following Scriptures that show examples of a pure heart.

- *Daniel*: "But Daniel made up his mind that he would not defile himself with the king's choice food or with the wine which he drank; so he sought permission from the commander of the officials that he might not defile himself." (Daniel 1:8)
- *Paul*: "But I do not consider my life of any account as dear to myself, so that I may finish my course and the ministry which I received from the Lord Jesus, to

testify solemnly of the gospel of the grace of God."
(Acts 20:24)

• *Christ*: "Jesus said to them, 'My food is to do the will of
   Him who sent Me and to accomplish His work.'" (John
   4:34)

Since God is conforming you to the image of Christ, trust
Him to develop this in you. We are not in this by ourselves,
but God is ruling over every event under heaven to bring it
about in our lives (Romans 8:28–29).

Third, continually deal with any disagreement with God. When
we realize that the "nearness of God is [our] good" (Psalm
73:28), we will purpose to walk in the light (1 John 1:7). This
involves walking openly, honestly, and transparently before
God and His truth. As God points out any sin in your life,
confess it and receive His gracious cleansing. God is for you
as you seek to restore your life to Him! Seek to always live
in the present moment.[6]

Fourth, learn to delight in God's presence. We can learn to
delight in God's presence by using the discipline of silence
and by praying throughout our day.

When you respond to the Spirit of God leading you into
silence, such obedience shows a faith that is willing to welcome God's control to quiet your anxious strivings. It also
shows your recognition that "trying too hard" can often be
counterproductive.

The prophet Jeremiah waited upon God quietly, and he
commended the practice in the book of Lamentations:

The Lord is good to those who wait for Him, to the person
who seeks Him. It is good that he waits silently for the salvation of the Lord. It is good for a man that he should bear

the yoke in his youth. Let him sit alone and be silent since He has laid it on him. (3:25-28)

We also can delight in God's presence by praying *through-out* our day. We may pray when we wake up, and/or when we go to bed. We may give thanks before each meal He has provided. But He is with us always and we can communicate with Him any time. Pray through your day in the light of God's presence being with you.

Visualize the truth of His being with you in every appointment, task, and responsibility. Anticipate meeting Him there even as you experience Him at this moment in prayer. Thank Him that every aspect of your life—all your relationships, work, routine errands, and hobbies—are of immense interest to your Lord. You might even consider scheduling special appointments or walks with the Lord with the express purpose of enjoying His presence.

Fifth, be alert to reminders of His presence. You might consider reviewing the following reminders each day for a couple of weeks in order to let them become ingrained in your thinking.

- Every task and responsibility can remind you that God's will is all that truly satisfies (John 4:34) and even the mundane is an opportunity to glorify Him (1 Corinthians 10:31).
- Every blessing can remind you that every good and perfect gift comes from above (James 1:17; compare 1 Corinthians 4:7).
- Every trial can remind you that He is ultimately in control of every event (Ephesians 1:11; Romans 8:28).

- Every temptation of fear and anxiety can be a reminder to seek Him and talk to Him about it (Psalm 34:4; Philippians 4:6–7).
- Every need or desire of your heart can be a reminder to come to Him for satisfaction (John 7:37–39).
- Every sin is a reminder to come to Him for cleansing (1 John 1:7–9). Be cautious to not stay on the ground after you have fallen.

God Is with You

A new believer came up to my mother one day at work. She exclaimed, "I thought about God today at work!" All her life she had worked every day, and God had never been a part of her work. A single thought about God may not be the ultimate in practicing God's presence, but God is pleased with the progress of your heart. Do not be discouraged with your apparent lack of progress but rather trust Him one day at a time and one moment at a time.

Jesus is our ultimate example as He modeled for us the abiding life (1 John 2:6). He lived in communion with the Father at all times—even during Jesus' time on earth.

Therefore Jesus answered and was saying to them, "Truly, truly, I say to you, the Son can do nothing of Himself, unless it is something He sees the Father doing; for whatever the Father does, these things the Son also does in like manner." (John 5:19)

So Jesus said, "When you lift up the Son of Man, then you will know that I am He, and I do nothing on My own initiative, but I speak these things as the Father taught Me.

And He who sent Me is with Me; He has not left Me alone, for I always do the things that are pleasing to Him." (John 8:28–29)

Let me encourage you again to take great comfort that if you are a believer, God is conforming you into the image of Christ—and one aspect of this image is practicing the presence of God.

There will be times of great difficulty when God may seem distant. Some have used the term "the dark night of the soul" to describe this state. Still, He is there. As Spurgeon once wrote, "When thy God hides His face, say not that He has forgotten thee. He is but tarrying a little while to make thee love Him better, and when He cometh, thou shalt have joy in the Lord and shalt rejoice with joy unspeakable."[7]

Tozer's words are a fitting conclusion: "We please Him most not by frantically trying to make ourselves good, but by throwing ourselves into His arms with all our imperfections and believing that He understands everything and loves us still."[8]

Notes

1. "Where God Ain't"; www.1Timothy4-13.com/files/chr_vik/wheregod. html. In public domain.

2. For more information about how to cultivate an awareness of God's presence, see Bill Thrasher, *How to Be a Soul Physician* (Seattle: Create-Space, 2010), 135–55. The book can be found at the author's website, www.victoriouspraying.com.

3. For the blessed results of God's hand being on one, look at Ezra 7:6, 9, 28; 8:18, 22, 31; Nehemiah 2:8, 18.

4. Stephen F. Olford, *Going Places with God* (Wheaton, Ill.: Victor, 1983), 20.

5. Robert Bakke, *Evangelical Beacon*, August 1996, 25.

6. To read further about this provision of continual cleansing, how to distinguish between true guilt and false guilt, how to distinguish between

Satan's accusations and the Holy Spirit's convictions, and how to live with a clear conscience before God, see Thrasher, *How to Be a Soul Physician*, 211–34, 239–58.

7. Quoted in Charles Colson, "My Soul's Dark Night," *Christianity Today*, December 2005, 80.

8. A. W. Tozer, "God Is Easy to Live With," *Best of A. W. Tozer*, book one, comp. Warren Wiersbe (Grand Rapids: Baker, 1978), 122.

10

God Is Omnipotent

HE HAS ALL POWER

IS ANYTHING TOO DIFFICULT for the Lord?" God asked two of His earliest followers, Abraham and Sarah (Genesis 18:14). Sometimes we wonder. We ask ourselves, *Can God handle* every *personal difficulty we face?*

The birth of a son seemed impossible to Sarah, who was clearly past childbearing age, and to Abraham, age one hundred. But by God's power Sarah conceived and Isaac was born. By the power of God nearly two thousand years later, a virgin would conceive and deliver a son named Jesus, being told by an angel, "Nothing will be impossible with God" (Luke 1:37). Jesus would be the promised Messiah, who would offer redemption for His people — and indeed the entire world — a way out of their greatest difficulty, separation from God and the sentence of death for their transgressions.

Amid all difficulties, God declares His ability to work both in judgment (cf. Jeremiah 32:17–18) and in salvation when He states, "With people this is impossible, but with God all things are possible" (Matthew 19:26). God's servants need to know and worship a God who can do "all things" and whose purpose cannot be thwarted (Job 42:2). Jesus' commission to disciple the nations comes only after His assertion that all authority and power in heaven and on earth are in His hands (Matthew 28:18).

The Almighty God

Among God's many names is one He Himself announced in ages past. To Abraham, God declared His name to be "God Almighty" and promised to establish His covenant with Abraham (Genesis 17:1–2). In response, Abraham fell on his face and listened to God's promises (vv. 3–8).

God also promises to be an almighty Father today to His sons and daughters (2 Corinthians 6:18). One day He will also demonstrate His unbounded power by being the almighty King who will judge all evil: "Hallelujah! For the Lord our God, the Almighty, reigns" (Revelation 19:6).

The Meaning of God's Omnipotence

God's omnipotence is a part of His very essence. All those in His creation have only the power that He has granted them. His power is greater than all of the collective power of all of His creatures. He alone has all power and is able to do all that He wills.

Are there any limits to His power? Yes, actually there are. God's power will always be exercised in harmony with

His attributes. So there are certain things God cannot do, for doing so would violate His character, the integrity of who He is. He cannot work inconsistently with His character.

In no way do we tell God what He can or cannot do. He is free to act as He wills. However, He has told us that there are certain things that He cannot do. In reality these limitations only magnify His power! What can't God do? Here are His limits:

- God cannot lie (Numbers 23:19; Titus 1:2; Hebrews 6:18).
- God cannot approve sin (Habakkuk 1:13).
- God cannot change His character (Malachi 3:6).
- God cannot deny Himself (2 Timothy 2:13); in other words, He cannot be unwise, unloving, or unfaithful.
- God cannot sin or entice one to sin (James 1:13).

God's Power on Display in Creation, His Providence, and His Salvation

God demonstrates His mighty power all around us *through His creation*. The Scriptures, especially Genesis 1–2 and the Psalms, tell us that at His command the universe and all of His creation came into being. Psalm 33 summarizes well His mighty work of creation: "By the word of the Lord the heavens were made, and by the breath of His mouth all their host. . . . He spoke, and it was done; He commanded, and it stood fast" (vv. 6, 9).

By His words He effortlessly created a universe so vast that at the speed of light—186,000 miles per second—it would take about one hundred thousand years to travel across our galaxy, the Milky Way Galaxy, which contains some 200 billion stars and other celestial objects. When you think that our galaxy is only one of billions of galaxies, you can begin to grasp the vastness of the universe that God created by His word.

In fact, His creation is a continual testimony of His "eternal power" (Romans 1:20). The only correct response to our omnipotent God's work in creation is one of gratitude (cf. Romans 1:21) and worship. Indeed, one day in heaven followers will bow down and exclaim, "Worthy are You, our Lord and our God, to receive glory and honor and power; for You created all things, and because of Your will they existed, and were created" (Revelation 4:11).

This omnipotence is not only seen in His creation but also in the sustaining and directing of it *by His providence.* In Christ "all things hold together" (Colossians 1:17) as He "upholds all things by the word of His power" (Hebrews 1:3). This involves His sustaining not only this vast universe but even each of our mental capacities, and circulatory, respiratory, and nervous systems, as He accomplishes His wise and loving purposes.

God's omnipotence appears also *in His plan of salvation.* As we noted, God brought the Messiah into the world through a miraculous virgin birth. In response to God's promise, Mary praised the "Mighty One" (Luke 1:49) and acknowledged His past mighty deeds (Luke 1:51). In Christ's life He displayed the power of God as Jesus miraculously provided food for the hungry multitudes, walked on water, stilled a storm, healed the sick, and raised the dead. The standard of God's power is seen in the raising of Christ from the dead as evident from the empty tomb.

It is this same power that can transform His followers from arrogant people into humble ones, from sinful individuals into genuinely spiritual people, and from warped thinkers into those knowing the wisdom of God.

God's Power on Display
in His Judgment

Because of the greatness of God's power, one day all His enemies will bow the knee to Him (Philippians 2:10–11; Psalm 66:3). When He comes again to judge the world and set up His kingdom, it will be with great power (Matthew 24:30). Those who know His power and have seen it will praise His judgments and salvation (see Revelation 19:1–3).

Descriptions of His Power

The descriptions of God's power throughout the Bible paint an awesome portrait of this awe-evoking Creator. The power of God is "eternal" (Romans 1:20). It cannot be exhausted and is always on display, for God "does not become weary or tired" (Isaiah 40:28) and "will neither slumber nor sleep" (Psalm 121:4). He is actively working (John 5:17) and even "works all things after the counsel of His will" (Ephesians 1:11). While He has not willed to do all that He is able to do (cf. Matthew 3:9; 26:53–54), His power will always be guided by His attributes.

God's power is supreme and unrivaled. The thought of all the mighty kings overthrowing His authority is only a laughable matter (Psalm 2:1–4). He is able to "nullify the counsel of the nations" and "frustrate the plans of the peoples" (Psalm 33:10), as no counsel or power can ultimately prevail over His will (Proverbs 21:30). One day all will acknowledge His supreme name (Philippians 2:10).

The proper response now to our omnipotent God is to worship (Revelation 4:11), fear (Matthew 10:28), and trust the God of all power. He is a God who can make us adequate for all tasks He calls us to (2 Corinthians 3:5–6) and will protect us to fulfill His will (Psalm 121; Proverbs 18:10; 1 Peter 1:5).

God's Power: The Key to Overcoming Our Fear of Opposition

God's power is mighty to save, and to triumph over our enemies. Our ultimate enemy is Satan, who wants to undermine every follower of Christ and make each follower move to the sidelines of the battle. A believer in Christ is in a spiritual battle against a well-organized host of angelic beings who have rebelled against God the Creator.

For this reason, it is necessary to depend on His strength. The apostle Paul tells us, writing in Ephesians,

> Finally, be strong in the Lord and in the strength of His might. Put on the full armor of God, so that you will be able to stand firm against the schemes of the devil. For our struggle is not against flesh and blood, but against the rulers, against the powers, against the world forces of this darkness, against the spiritual forces of wickedness in the heavenly places. (6:10–12)

The Lord tells us that we are not to be ignorant of Satan's schemes (2 Corinthians 2:11). Table 5 provides a sample of some of Satan's schemes. Be alert to these schemes, but also look to your all-powerful God to work for you in the opposite ways!

Table 5
The Power of God and
the Power of Satan

Bible Passage	Satan	All-Powerful God
Acts 5:3; 1 Timothy 4:1	Satan tempts us to lie and deceive.	God seeks to make us men and women of truth.
1 Corinthians 7:5	Satan tempts us to immorality.	God seeks to make us men and women of moral integrity.
Revelation 12:4–10	Satan accuses and slanders us and promotes this attitude in our relationships.	God seeks to affirm, lovingly convict, and promote speech characterized by love.
Genesis 3:1–5	Satan promotes doubt in God's character and His Word.	God seeks to empower us to believe Him and His Word.
1 Samuel 15:23; 1 Timothy 3:6	Satan promotes pride and selfishness.	God promotes humility.
1 Chronicles 21:1–8; Matthew 16:21–23	Satan encourages reliance on human resource and human wisdom.	God promotes full confidence in His perfect power and wisdom.
Daniel 7:25	Satan seeks to "wear out the saints." (This verse is speaking of the antichrist whom Satan empowers.)	God leads us to true rest and refreshment.
Ephesians 4:26–27	Satan seeks to stir up anger in order to gain an advantage for spiritual, emotional, and physical harm.	God comforts our hearts and promotes love and forgiveness.
Acts 5:3; John 13:2	Satan puts wicked purposes into people's minds and hearts.	God puts loving purposes into our minds and hearts.
Deuteronomy 18:10	Satan seeks to harm innocent children.	God welcomes children to love and perfect them.

In regard to the last scheme, child sacrifice was often associated with idolatry. The Bible speaks of demonic activity behind idolatry even today when one embraces an idol in their life — a hobby, job, etc. — one will sacrifice the spiritual well-being of their children to this idol. As we place ourselves under the authority of our all-powerful God, we can experience His victory over Satan and his demonic forces. As James writes, "Submit therefore to God. Resist the devil and he will flee from you."[1]

God's Power and the Fear of Men

For many Christians, the fear of what people may do or say (Proverbs 29:25) matches their fear of Satan's opposition. Different terms are used to describe the snare or "trap" of fearing men. This fear sometimes expresses itself in *people pleasing*, bowing to *peer pressure*, and *codependency*. God wants us to be sensitive and thoughtful to others but also free to make the right choice about who is to be our Lord. Paul asked two legitimate questions, ones we should ask as well. "Am I now seeking the favor of men, or of God? Or am I striving to please men? If I were still trying to please men, I would not be a bond-servant of Christ" (Galatians 1:10).

God's Word encourages us not to fear man. God's people are told not to fear man but rather to focus on the acts of their omnipotent God (Deuteronomy 7:17–26). Four other key passages remind us that pleasing people makes little sense when God is with us:

No man will be able to stand before you all the days of your life. Just as I have been with Moses, I will be with you; I will not fail you or forsake you. (Joshua 1:5)

"I, even I, am He who comforts you. Who are you that you are afraid of man who dies and of the son of man who is made like grass, that you have forgotten the Lord your Maker, who stretched out the heavens and laid the foundations of the earth, that you fear continually all day long because of the fury of the oppressor, as he makes ready to destroy? But where is the fury of the oppressor?

"The exile will soon be set free, and will not die in the dungeon, nor will his bread be lacking. For I am the Lord your God, who stirs up the sea and its waves roar (the Lord of hosts is His name)." (Isaiah 51:12–15)

Do not fear those who kill the body but are unable to kill the soul; but rather fear Him who is able to destroy both soul and body in hell. (Matthew 10:28)

Who is there to harm you if you prove zealous for what is good? But even if you should suffer for the sake of righteousness, you are blessed. And do not fear their intimidation, and do not be troubled. (1 Peter 3:13–14)[2]

The Call to Experience God's Power

As Jesus addressed the seven churches of Revelation 2 and 3, which church received the most severe rebuke? It was the church of Laodicea, characterized as "lukewarm." What is lukewarmness? Jesus gave us the answer when He quoted this church: "'I am rich, and have become wealthy, and have need of nothing'" (Revelation 3:17). The condition of this church was self-sufficiency. That attitude is nauseating to the heart of Christ, and so He declared, "I will spit you out of My mouth" (v. 16).

The area of Laodicia was known for its banking center, manufacturing of clothes, and medical expertise; however, those in its church were advised to come to Christ to buy gold, to clothe themselves with His garments, and to anoint their eyes with the eye salve that He would provide (v. 18). They needed to respond to His knock at the door and invite Him to dine with them (v. 20). The truth of our inadequacy is the consistent testimony of Scripture.

According to the Scriptures, our power comes from God alone. Twice Paul tells those in the church at Corinth to focus on experiencing God's power:

> Not that we are adequate in ourselves to consider any-thing as coming from ourselves, but our adequacy is from God, who also made us adequate as servants of a new covenant, not of the letter but of the Spirit; for the letter kills, but the Spirit gives life. (2 Corinthians 3:5–6)

> But we have this treasure in earthen vessels, so that the surpassing greatness of the power will be of God and not from ourselves. (2 Corinthians 4:7)

Five Life-Changing Prayers

With the call to rely on God's power for our daily needs, here are five biblical prayers for power you may use.

1.*"Lord, let me experience the power of Your resurrection"* (Philippians 3:10).

This was both the apostle Paul's ambition for his own life (Philippians 3:10) and for other believers (Ephesians 1:19–23). What does it mean to experience the power of the res-urrection? First, it involves the experience of victory over sin and death as we appropriate our identification with Christ.[3] It also involves experiencing victory in the midst of your apparent defeats. When Christ was in the grave, it looked as though the enemies of unrighteousness had won. However, God was winning a victory in the midst of this apparent defeat and afterward came the resurrection![4]

2. *"Lord, show me the meaning of the words, 'Apart from Me you can do nothing'"* (John 15:5).

This is the consistent testimony of Scripture: " 'Not by might nor by power, but by My Spirit,' says the Lord of hosts" (Zechariah 4:6). Do not be content to just quote this, but come to God and ask Him what it means that *nothing* can be done apart from abiding in the vine, as Jesus declared in John 15:5.

We can do much activity independent of Him. In fact during one difficult time in my life, I discovered that I really did not believe John 15:5. Do you believe it? Would you be willing to let your omnipotent God teach you the truth of this verse? Each day for us is a day of placing our faith in Christ and watching Him work (Galatians 2:20). It is for this reason that when Paul gave his mission report he spoke of what Christ had done, not as pious words but as an accurate cumulative effect of his daily dependence upon his Lord (see Romans 15:18).

3. *"Lord, show me what it means to labor in Your strength"* (see also Colossians 1:29).

It is easy to get confused by various teachings on the Christian life. One week we are encouraged to diligently seek God and pursue the spiritual disciplines. The next week we are told that the problem is that we are trying too hard and need to relax and let God have His way. Who is correct?

The Christian life is a labor. God does want our best effort as we "do [our] work heartily, as for the Lord rather than for men" (Colossians 3:23). However, there is a difference between laboring, even laboring for the Lord, and laboring "according to His power" (Colossians 1:29). One can leave you not only tired physically but also spiritually. The other can leave you tired but also refreshed by your fellowship with Christ, even as you cast your cares and concerns upon the Lord (1 Peter 5:7).

Put your finger on Colossians 1:29 and ask Him to teach you to labor in His strength in the midst of all of your responsibilities and concerns today. He is an omnipotent God but also a kind and gentle teacher.[5]

4. *"Lord, show me what it means for You to be strong in my weakness"* (2 Corinthians 12:9).

While suffering through some infirmity, Paul pleaded with God to remove it. God answered, "My grace is sufficient for you, for power is perfected in weakness." Paul accepted that answer and saw the connection: through weakness "the power of Christ may dwell in me." Therefore the apostle was ready to endure not only weaknesses but also "insults . . . distresses . . . persecutions [and] difficulties, for Christ's sake; for when I am weak, then I am strong" (2 Corinthians 12:9–10).

God can bless us with weaknesses that humble us in order to experience more of His gracious enablement. Thus James alludes to Psalm 138:6 when he writes, "But He gives a greater grace. Therefore it says, 'God is opposed to the proud, but gives grace to the humble'" (James 4:6).

5. *"Lord, show me how I grieve and quench Your Spirit"* (Ephesians 4:30; 1 Thessalonians 5:19).

One of the kind expressions of God's power is His liberating convicting work! Let God search your heart.

Search me, O God, and know my heart; try me and

know my anxious thoughts; and see if there be any hurt-
ful way in me, and lead me in the everlasting way.
(Psalm 139:23–24)

Ask God to illuminate areas of your life that show attitudes of self-sufficiency, self-indulgence, lack of obedience,
excessive busyness, and a hurried spirit. Ask Him to reveal
whether there is a lack of unity with anyone with whom you
need to reconcile (Romans 12:18). Remember that His convicting work is kind and loving and far different from the
harassing accusations of the Evil One.[6]

God's Power to Help Others

All who know Jesus as their Savior are called to serve
others. Whatever your ministry, the power of God offers you
strength to accomplish His purposes. We are not adequate by
ourselves (2 Corinthians 3:5). He alone can equip us for life
and ministry in this way. As He works, the focus is to be on
Him and not on the vessel that He uses (2 Corinthians 4:7).
He continually warned His people against trusting in themselves — their training, preparation, and resources. In the time
of King David, the psalmist reminded Israel that the king's
ultimate strength lay not in his militia but in his God: "The
king is not saved by a mighty army; a warrior is not delivered
by great strength. A horse is a false hope for victory" (Psalm
33:16–17). Trust God alone to provide opportunities and even
to change lives. He is able to open doors that no one can shut
(Revelation 3:8)! A previously closed door in some cases may
later become an open door. This was the case in regard to
Paul's ministry in Asia (1 Corinthians 16:9). An open door
does not necessarily mean that there will be no difficulties,

but it does mean that we can look to Him and find and experience His sufficiency in the midst of these challenges.

Only God alone can produce obedience that comes from the heart. It is for this reason that Paul spoke about what "God had done" through his ministry (Acts 21:19; see also Romans 15:18).

Learn to pray to the God who is able. The Scriptures tell us His ability has no limits. (For a New Testament perspective, see the feature "He Is Able" below.)

He Is Able

Each of the following verses refers to one aspect of God's ability. Pray in confidence to the God . . .

- who is able to keep His promises—Romans 4:21.
- who is able to make you stand firm and establish you—Romans 14:4.
- who is "able to do far more abundantly beyond all" you can ask or think—Ephesians 3:20.
- who is able to guard what you have entrusted to Him—2 Timothy 1:12.
- who is "able to keep you from stumbling, and to make you stand in the presence of His glory blameless with great joy"—Jude 24.

Witnesses to God's Power

Though not a believer, Gamaliel verbalized the logic that there is no way to fight against God and win (Acts 5:34, 38–39).

In a day of trouble, King Jehoshaphat declared that "power and might are in Your hand so that no one can stand against You" (2 Chronicles 20:6).

Two apostles also testify to His mighty power. Peter writes that God's divine power has given us everything we need to experience fellowship with Him — "life" — and to reflect Him — "godliness" (see 2 Peter 1:3). We can trust His omnipotent power to protect us to fulfill His purposes (1 Peter 1:5). John writes that a believer is in the hands of an all-powerful God who is "greater than all" (John 10:29)!

There is no reason to boast in our might but rather to join the heavenly choir that is singing the praises of His power (Revelation 4:11; 5:12). It is a great privilege to know and worship an omnipotent God who is for us.

What then shall we say to these things? If God is for us, who is against us? (Romans 8:31)

Notes

1. For more insight on this topic, see Bill and Penny Thrasher, *Putting God Back into the Holidays* (Chicago: Moody, 2010), 246–49. Satan's schemes and influence are discussed in the context of the Halloween celebration.

2. For more insight into what it means to be free from the fear of man, see Bill Thrasher, *How to Be a Soul Physician* (Seattle: CreateSpace, 2010), 67–86. The book can be found at the author's website, www.victorious praying.com.

3. For practical insight in experiencing this, see Ibid., 101–30.

4. For more on how to experience victory in the midst of apparent defeats, see Bill Thrasher, *A Journey to Victorious Praying* (Chicago: Moody, 2003), 17–38.

5. For additional practical insights on laboring in God's strength, see *How to Be a Soul Physician*, 135–55.

6. To learn more about these contrasts see Ibid., 223–28

Part Four

A PERFECTLY HOLY, RIGHTEOUS, FAITHFUL, AND LOVING PERSON

11

God Is Holy

HE ALONE IS TRULY BEAUTIFUL

THE EARLY CHURCH made membership a lengthy process that could take two or three years. The lives of the interested parishioners were carefully examined. Church leaders wanted to make sure that prospective members were leading holy lives.

The effort was seen not only as a protection for the pre-Constantinian church but also for the seeker, since being a member of the church might even cost them their life. David Neff observes that the present church has adopted the wide-door strategy of retail marketing whose doors automatically open wide to any potential customer. Neff asks, "Whom should we emulate? The pre-Constantinian Apostolic constitutions or Target?"[1] He also observes that it is not fair to frame the question in this way. The early church did welcome the needy, slaves, orphans, women, and the sick.

Neff goes on to point out the difference between welcoming and inclusion. When we include the unrepentant as full-fledged members of the church, it loses its identity. The result is having nothing of real value into which those of need can be welcomed.

Caroline Westerhoff in *Good Fences: The Boundaries of Hospitality* notes that "Jesus says that narrow doors and gates offer the only sure and safe entrance into God's realm of life. Gates that swing too wide and doors that open too fast do not give us the opportunity to slow down and decide what is important before we make our choices."[2]

The Meaning of God's Holiness

The apostle John not only states that "God is love" (1 John 4:8, 16) but also that "God is Light, and in Him there is no darkness at all" (1 John 1:5). "Light" is used to refer to the revelation of His holiness. The absence of any darkness refers to His complete separation from all sin. John frequently refers to darkness as sin (see John 1:5; 3:19; 12:35; 1 John 1:5–6; 2:8–9, 11).

God is holy in that He is not only "set apart" or exalted above all of His creation but also separate from all moral evil and sin. This also means that He is infinite in moral excellence and purity. For this reason the Scripture speaks of the "beauty of the Lord" (Psalm 27:4). You can adore God who is truly perfect in every way, and as you gaze intently at Him, you observe no flaw or imperfection in His character.

His holiness motivates His love for what is right, good, and pure. His love and devotion for what is truly beautiful and perfect give Him a corresponding perfect hatred for what is opposed to it. He can "take no pleasure in wicked-ness" because there is absolutely no evil in Him (Psalm 5:4). In fact, Proverbs 6:17–19 lists seven things "the Lord hates," including wicked plans. Those seven are "haughty eyes, a lying tongue, and hands that shed innocent blood, a heart that devises wicked plans, feet that run rapidly to evil, a false witness who utters lies, and one who spreads strife among brothers."

Our holy God also hates hypocritical religious celebra-tions (Amos 5:21–22). As you respond to His holy love, He will develop in you a love for Him that is also accompanied by a hatred of evil (Psalm 97:10) and that in no way rejoices in unrighteousness (1 Corinthians 13:6). Habakkuk tells us His eyes are too pure to approve evil (1:13).

In His holiness He can never encourage sin or be blamed for it in any way. James writes, "Let no one say when he is tempted, 'I am being tempted by God'; for God cannot be tempted by evil, and He Himself does not tempt anyone" (James 1:13).

When we are tempted, we are not to follow our forefather Adam and blame God as he did — "The woman whom You gave to be with me, she gave me from the tree, and I ate" (Genesis 3:12). We will make progress only when we run to God in our temptation and seek His aid and accept full responsibility for our sin. James declares that each of us "is tempted when he is carried away and enticed by his own lust" (James 1:14).

The Testimony of Scripture

In a stunning vision, Isaiah beheld the Lord seated on a throne, "lofty and exalted," and listened as one angel "called out to another and said, 'Holy, Holy, Holy, is the Lord of hosts, the whole earth is full of His glory'" (Isaiah 6:1, 3).

In the Scriptures, each person of our triune God is described as holy — Father (John 17:11), Son (Acts 3:14), and Spirit (Ephesians 4:30). "There is no one holy like the Lord" (1 Samuel 2:2), for He alone is holy (Revelation 15:4).

The Scriptures also tell us the works of God flow from His holy character. Out of His holiness, He creates (Isaiah 43:15), redeems (Isaiah 43:14), chooses (Isaiah 49:7), and revives the hearts of the holy and contrite (Isaiah 57:15), and one day He will glorify His people (Isaiah 60:9). Out of His holiness, He speaks (Psalm 60:6) and swears to fulfill His promises of blessing (Psalm 89:35–37) and judgment (Amos 4:2).

While even saints in heaven wait for the complete vindication of His holy name (Revelation 6:10), it has been and will be manifested and vindicated (Numbers 16:5–7). Because His throne is holy (Psalm 47:8), those who fail to treat Him as holy will be judged (Leviticus 10:13; 1 Samuel 6:20). Even Moses was disciplined for failing to treat God as holy in his act of disobedience before the people (Numbers 20:12). When God's people live in bondage, His name is profaned in the world (Ezekiel 36:20). God is concerned for His holy name (Ezekiel 36:21). Out of jealously for His holiness, He will restore and bless His people (Deuteronomy 26:15; Ezekiel 28:25; 36:22; 39:25). God tells us that there will be a future day when all will know that "I am the Lord, the Holy One" (Ezekiel 39:7).

God's Holiness Revealed on Earth

There is no misunderstanding of His holiness in heaven, where it elicits continuous praise (Isaiah 6:3; Revelation 4:8).

However, here on earth God goes to great lengths to educate us about His holiness. The detailed revelation of the tabernacle and the temple is a part of His Scriptures. The separation of the holy and the most holy place (Exodus 26:33; 1 Kings 6:16, 19) reveals to God's people of all ages that He cannot be approached without His gracious provisions. The provision of the detailed sacrificial system communicates to us the necessity of a payment for sin in order to approach a holy God (Leviticus 1–7). God appointed a priesthood to mediate these sacrifices (Leviticus 8–10). The Law had not only a regulatory purpose to guide God's people but also a revelatory purpose, proclaiming for all time God's holiness.

The tabernacle and sacrifices reveal the necessity and magnitude of the accomplishment of the death of Christ. Isaiah described our separation from God's holy presence and the need for a Savior to reconcile us to our Creator: "Behold, the Lord's hand is not so short that it cannot save; nor is His ear so dull that it cannot hear. But your iniquities have made a separation between you and your God, and your sins have hidden His face from you so that He does not hear" (Isaiah 59:1–2).

Later, Jesus Christ would declare that He alone provides the way to God (John 14:6; Acts 4:12). He is the *mediator* to bring us to a holy God (1 Timothy 2:5). For this reason it is possible to approach our holy God with a "full assurance of faith."

Therefore, brethren, since we have confidence to enter the holy place by the blood of Jesus, by a new and living way which He inaugurated for us through the veil, that is, His flesh, and since we have a great priest over the house of God, let us draw near with a sincere heart in full assurance of faith, having our hearts sprinkled clean from an evil conscience and our bodies washed with pure water. (Hebrews 10:19–22)

God's Desire for Holiness in His People

God's commands are always for our good (Deuteronomy 10:13), and this involves the command to be holy (Leviticus 11:44; 1 Peter 1:15). Sin and idolatry "pains" (Psalm 78:41), "grieves" (Ephesians 4:30), and "profanes" the holy name of God (Leviticus 20:3; 22:32), and sin "injures" our own lives (Proverbs 8:36) and withholds good from us (Jeremiah 5:25). It is for this reason that the Bible tells us to pursue holiness (Hebrews 12:14). What pains and grieves Him also hurts and injures our life. His glory is for our eternal good!

God not only commands us to be holy but works on our behalf to make this happen. He chooses us so that we can become "holy and blameless" before Him (Ephesians 1:4; Colossians 1:22). He has also *redeemed* and *reconciled* us that we might be holy—set apart as "a people for His own possession" (Titus 2:14; Deuteronomy 7:6). In this sense, in Christ He has already sanctified us as His holy people (1 Corinthians 1:2). His glorious salvation also involves our regeneration, which makes us new creatures who can live holy lives (Ephesians 4:24).

Our holy God controls all the events of each of our lives to allow only the suffering and trials that work for our true good (Romans 8:28–29). Remember that it is His holy name that evokes awe (Psalm 111:9), that allows us to "serve Him without fear, in holiness and righteousness before Him all our days" (Luke 1:74–75). The purifying fear of God replaces the paralyzing fear of man as we live before a holy God. Our holy and loving God is so devoted to us that He will even discipline us so that we may "share His holiness" (Hebrews 12:10; cf. 1 Peter 4:17–18).

In addition, the future hope of the destruction of this world and the creation of a new heaven and new earth is to prompt us to live holy lives (2 Peter 3:11). One day each believer will experience ultimate holiness, being sanctified entirely — body, soul, and spirit (1 Thessalonians 5:23–24).

Knowing Him

His Holiness in Us

When we begin to understand God is holy, we live differently. Here are several outcomes—evidences really—that show we recognize our God is Holy:

1. *We become humble.* Realizing we are under condemnation before a holy Creator, we are humbled.
2. *We become grateful and confident.* God is holy, yet in Christ we have full acceptance and immediate access to our holy God. This creates gratitude and confidence within us.
3. *We worship our holy God.* We're invited to "glory in His holy name" (1 Chronicles 16:10).
4. *We recognize and quickly deal with our sins.* A person who knows the holy God becomes sensitive to sin in his life.
5. *We begin to trust Him more.* His holiness is a ground of trust when we are perplexed. What we do not understand we commit to a holy God who does what is right.
6. *We move toward joyful surrender.* When we see God as holy, we present the totality of our lives to God.

What Happens When
We Grasp That God Is Holy?

One day God will reveal His holiness for all the nations to see (Ezekiel 28:25). But as we begin to understand that we serve a holy God, certain attitudes and actions change in our lives. Here is what happens as we begin to grasp that God is holy.

First, we become humble. A glimpse of God's holiness will produce a deep humility in us, as we recognize that in and of ourselves we stand under His holy condemnation—and yet He has chosen to redeem us through His Son, Jesus. Even one impure thought, one ill-advised word, or one moment of unrighteous anger is enough for God to sentence us to an eternal hell; and all we could say is that He has done what is right.

The good news is that the "high and exalted One who lives forever, whose name is Holy" dwells in a "high and holy place, and also with the contrite and lowly of spirit in order to revive the spirit of the lowly and to revive the heart of the contrite" (Isaiah 57:15). As His holiness draws us to acknowledge our sin, we can also enjoy His holy presence and have our heart revived!

Second, we become grateful and confident. As young children we must learn to stand on two legs to remain balanced. As Christians, on one leg we humbly acknowledge our complete and total need for Christ; apart from His gracious work, we stand condemned. On the other, we accept gratefully His gracious offer to "draw near with confidence to the throne of grace" (Hebrews 4:16).

In Christ we can find full acceptance and immediate access to our holy God. A believer stands in God's grace

(Romans 5:2) and has the confidence to enter the Holy of Holies at any time. (See Hebrews 10:19–22 and also Matthew 27:51, where upon Jesus' death, "the veil [curtain] of the temple was torn in two," giving man symbolic access to the Holy of Holies and the presence of God.)

Third, we worship our holy God. Scripture tells us to "glory in His holy name" (1 Chronicles 16:10), to worship Him (1 Chronicles 16:29), to give thanks to His holy name (1 Chronicles 16:35), to sing praise to Him (Psalm 71:22), and to exalt Him (Psalm 99:9). When we understand that God is holy, we bless His holy name (Psalm 103:1), "rejoice in the Holy One of Israel" (Isaiah 29:19), and "sanctify the Holy One of Jacob" (Isaiah 29:23).

The revelation of the only One who is truly perfect demands a response of worship. In His kindness He allows us to enjoy His perfection as we worship Him in an imperfect world and long one day to serve and worship Him day and night (Revelation 7:15).

Fourth, we recognize and quickly deal with our sins. One who is beginning to sense the holiness of God develops the pattern of walking in the "Light" before God (1 John 1:7).

Such open, honest, and transparent living before God involves confessing our sins as God points them out to us and living in agreement with Him (1 John 1:9). This is the opposite of covering our sins, which results in the removal of God's prospering hand (Proverbs 28:13).

Fifth, we begin to trust Him more. It has often been said that at times you may find it hard to "trace the hand of God" in your life, but you can always "trust the heart of God." His holiness is a ground of trust when we are perplexed. We can say, "God, I do not fully understand, but I know You are holy."

Such is the confidence of the psalmist who acknowledges

God's holiness — "Your way, O God, is holy . . ." (Psalm 77:13) — even in the midst of the day of his trouble (Psalm 77:2). When God does not answer our prayers for deliverance in order to achieve His higher purpose, we can still trust in His holiness (Psalm 22:2–3).

Sixth, we move toward joyful surrender. What does it mean to be holy? The word *holy* means "to be set apart." We are living a holy life when we present the totality of our lives to God. One of the reasons for Christ's death was to deliver us from our slavery to our own self-will. It is for this reason that apart from Christ all of us can be described as slaves to sin (Romans 6:17) because the only life we could ever live is a self-willed life. Christ's death liberates us to not go on presenting the members of our bodies to sin but to "present [ourselves] to God . . . and all [our] members as instruments of righteousness" (Romans 6:13).

Many "successful" people are very bored in life because they have never found a way to involve all of their capacities, even in their productive and seemingly prestigious lives. God in His kindness tells us that every part of our being can be presented to Him and enjoy His fellowship. What if all the people reading this book were to present the totalities of their lives to God? We could significantly impact the world in our sphere as God will always use and take care of what has been committed to Him!

God encourages us to consecrate ourselves to Him because He is holy (Leviticus 20:7). He encourages us to surrender our plans and talents to Him and let Him fight our battles (cf. Deuteronomy 23:14). We cannot serve a holy God and another god at the same time (Joshua 24:14).

A Time for Surrender

Would you be willing to get on your knees and put your finger on Romans 12:1 and tell God that you do not want to get up from your knees until you have obeyed this verse? "Present your bodies a living and holy sacrifice, acceptable to God, which is your spiritual service of worship," the apostle writes. Put every part of your life into His hands; let Him help you discover and develop every capacity within you.

Then watch Him work on your behalf one day at a time, one moment at a time. He has made it possible to live a holy life by making it possible for you to joyfully surrender your life to a holy God!

Notes

1. David Neff, "Please Fence Me In," *Christianity Today*, December 2004.
2. Caroline Westerhoff, *Good Fences* (New York: Morehouse, 2004), 31; as quoted by Neff in "Please Fence Me in," *Christianity Today*, December 2004.

12

God Is Righteous

HE SITS UPON HIS THRONE JUDGING RIGHTEOUSLY

DAVID UNDERSTOOD that the mighty God reigns in righteousness on His throne when he wrote to the Lord in gratitude: "When my enemies turn back, they stumble and perish before You. For You have maintained my just cause; You have sat on the throne judging righteously" (Psalm 9:3–4).

Righteousness is that aspect of God's holiness that is displayed in the moral equity of His governing of the world. He always acts consistently with His character. It is not technically correct to say that "righteousness requires God to do this," for that would place some standard above God. He is free to act as He wills, and all He does will be righteous.

Righteousness:
It's in God's Character

Jesus addresses the Father as "righteous Father" (John 17:25). Righteousness belongs to God alone (Isaiah 45:24; Daniel 9:7), though Jesus, God incarnate, is called the "Holy and Righteous One" (Acts 3:14). Only God is "righteous in all His ways" (Psalm 145:17). The prophets write that God "will do no injustice" (Zephaniah 3:5) and is the very "habitation of righteousness" (Jeremiah 50:7).

God's righteous character is imprinted on His law (Psalm 19:9; Romans 7:12), and His wisdom yields the fruit of righteousness (James 3:18). His Scriptures are designed to train His people in His righteousness (2 Timothy 3:16), and He Himself will be righteous and will fulfill all the promises of His Word (Nehemiah 9:8).

The revelation of God's righteous acts provoked wicked Pharaoh to temporarily acknowledge the Lord as "the righteous one" (Exodus 9:27). The proper response to this attribute is to continually give glory to Him (Isaiah 24:16), give thanks to Him (Psalm 7:17), joyfully sing to Him (Psalm 51:14), and to proclaim and continually declare the good news of His righteousness (Psalms 35:28; 40:9).

A Standard We Cannot Achieve

God's righteousness demands perfect and continual heart obedience to His holy law. "For Moses writes that the man who practices the righteousness which is based on law shall live by that righteousness" (Romans 10:5).

This is a standard to which we can never attain. The Scriptures consistently testify that in God's sight "no man living is righteous" (Psalm 143:2); "Indeed, there is not a righteous man on earth who continually does good and who never sins" (Ecclesiastes 7:20); and "there is none righteous, not even one" (Romans 3:10).

Christ Himself said He did not come to call people who thought they were righteous (Matthew 9:13), and He rejected those who had only an outward show of righteousness (Matthew 6:1; 23:27–28; Luke 18:9). He warned His listeners, "Unless your righteousness surpasses that of the scribes and Pharisees, you will not enter the kingdom of heaven" (Matthew 5:20).

God's Righteousness and His Wrath

For those who question their need for the gift of righteousness, the Bible records God's own righteousness and our lack of righteousness in several ways. *First, God demonstrates that He is righteous by imprinting His eternal moral law on the conscience of every person He creates* (Romans 2:14–15). His moral law is always for the ultimate good of His people (Deuteronomy 10:13). It is to protect us from harming ourselves and others and to point us to the best path of life. But we cannot measure up to His standard. We are "all under sin" (Romans 3:9–10).

Second, He makes clear that His righteousness requires a payment for the sins of men and women. His righteousness demands that sin be punished by His wrath. In fact, His very Word states that justifying the wicked is an abomination to the Lord (Proverbs 17:15)! How could God offer His gracious justification to Old Testament saints like Abraham (Genesis 15:6)? How can He now "justify the ungodly" (Romans 4:5), and it not be an abomination? He did it in the past and does it in the present on the basis of Christ's work.

Several words are needed to describe the accomplishments of Christ's death. One of these words is "propitiation." This is the Godward side of the cross. God's righteousness is satisfied by Christ's payment for sin, and He is graciously free to impute Christ's righteousness to our account. It is for this reason that Christ's death "demonstrated His righteousness" so that He could be both "just and the justifier" (Romans 3:25–26).

In the same way, it is Christ's propitiation that allows the believer to enjoy the continual cleansing of the blood of Christ. God does not desire us to sin, but if we do sin, we are to agree with God's conviction and confess it. His response of cleansing us is a righteous response that allows us to enjoy fellowship with Him (1 John 1:9). It would not be righteous if there had not been a just payment for this sin.[1]

Third, God expresses His wrath against sin in righteousness by showing His patience. Judgment is said to be God's "unusual . . . extraordinary work" (Isaiah 28:21). He will pour out His wrath on the unrepentant (see Psalm 7:11–12). Yet He is slow to wrath (Nahum 1:3) and yearns for people to escape His judgment. For this reason He sent His prophets to warn people to flee from the coming wrath (Matthew 3:7). The mission of the Messiah's first coming was not to judge the world but to bring salvation from judgment (John 3:17). God's patience and kindness is designed to lead us to repentance (Romans 2:4–5), for He does not wish for any to perish (2 Peter 3:9).

God's wrath is not to be understood in human terms as a fit of passion, but it is rather His loving and righteous reaction to sin and His determination to judge it. He is never unrighteous and will always judge in righteousness (Revelation 19:11). The judge of all the earth will always do right (Genesis 18:25). People may look at the world today and conclude that there is not a righteous judge. It appears that many people profit from unethical oppressive behavior and the innocent are not always vindicated. However, the final judgment is said to be a "revelation of the righteous judgment of God" (Romans 2:5).

Fourth, a day of righteous judgment awaits. God has manifested His righteous judgment in the past. Notable examples are the flood in Noah's day and Sodom and Gomorrah. He is also displaying His wrath in the present day by giving people over to their sin, removing His restraint, and letting their sin intensify itself (Romans 1:18–32).

There also will be a future display of God's wrath during the tribulation period (Revelation 6:17) as well as at the great white throne judgment.

Any person who has violated God's moral standards — any adultery, fornication, lying, theft, murder, unrighteous use of authority, idol worshiping, or any oppression of the needy — and has not repented will be judged (Malachi 3:5; cf. Hebrews 13:4). The Bible makes clear that all of us have violated His standards (Romans 3:23). His wrath will be against all ungodliness and unrighteousness (cf. Romans 1:18). One may be a very powerful man or woman who has a great evil empire, but God hates all who love violence (Psalm 11:5). No one will be able to stand before the Almighty on the day of judgment on their own merit (Revelation 20:15; Nahum 1:6).

Judgment will be exercised with no partiality (Romans 2:11) and will take into account the secrets of man's heart (Romans 2:16). It will also take into account the revelation that one has received (Romans 2:12). All men have at least received the revelation of creation and conscience (Romans 2:14–15) and are left with no excuse (Romans 1:20).

There is only one Lawgiver and Judge (James 4:12). Final judgment has not been placed into the hands of man but rather into the hands of an eternal righteous God. Evil will not be tolerated forever. Unrighteousness will not win or even profit in the long run. The truth of God's pouring out His wrath on the unrepentant not only demonstrates that He is righteous but also serves as an encouragement for God's suffering servants to faithfully persevere in the midst of injustice (Revelation 14:12; cf. Psalm 73:17).

God Offers the Gift of Righteousness

In the midst of such rebellion and pending punishment, the righteous God offers "the gift of righteousness" that can be received by faith (Romans 5:17). We do not have "a righteousness of [our] own derived from the Law, but [a righteousness] which is through faith in Christ, the righteousness which comes from God on the basis of faith" (Philippians 3:9). In other words this righteousness is not based on what we can do but rather on what Christ has done.

Everyone is in need of this gift that only our righteous God can give. He bestows it freely, based on the anguish or toilsome labor of Christ (see Isaiah 53:11). This is the only way that one can be righteous before God. It is not based on any religious practice or performance (Romans 4:9–15) but solely on the merits of Christ's righteousness. Thus God "made Him who knew no sin to be sin on our behalf, so that we might become the righteousness of God in Him" (2 Corinthians 5:21).

Our Responses

We are not saved by our righteousness (Titus 3:5) but by His gift of righteousness. However, we are to practice righteousness (1 John 3:7), pursue it with other believers (2 Timothy 2:22), seek it (Zephaniah 2:3; Matthew 6:33), and hunger and thirst for it (Matthew 5:6). These are to be our responses to God's gift of righteousness.

One of the jobs of a godly father is to tenderly plead with his children to live righteously. Thus Abraham would urge, even "command his children . . . to keep the way of the Lord by doing righteousness and justice" (Genesis 18:19).

His Rewards for Our Works of Faith

God will reward our righteous actions, both in this day and during the final judgment. Every believer will be tempted to "lose heart in doing good," and the key to overcoming this is to remember that we serve a righteous God (Galatians 6:9).

God instituted the principle of sowing and reaping. The one who "sows in tears" will one day "reap with joyful shouting" (Psalm 126:5). For this reason, "The merciful man does himself good, but the cruel man does himself harm" (Proverbs 11:17). The wicked will not prosper in the end, but the one "who sows righteousness gets a true reward" (Proverbs 11:18).

Jesus assured His followers that any sacrifice they made for Him in love would be rewarded (Matthew 19:29). Not even the smallest gesture—even a cup of cold water given in His name—would go unnoticed or forgotten (Mark 9:41)! This is grounded in His attributes of righteousness, as "God is not unjust so as to forget your work and the love which you have shown toward His name" (Hebrews 6:10).

Isaiah lets us in on a private and prophetic conversation between the Father and the Son:

He said to Me, "You are My Servant, Israel, in Whom I will show My glory." But I said, "I have toiled in vain, I have spent My strength for nothing and vanity; yet surely the justice due to Me is with the Lord, and My reward with My God." (Isaiah 49:3–4)

The Messiah was tempted to feel He had toiled in vain as He experienced the resistance of the arrogant religious establishment, the misunderstanding of His own family, and His own disciples who would eventually betray Him in His hour of need. However, He surrendered this temptation to His righteous Father whom He knew would reward Him!

God assured even a first-century slave that he would "receive back from the Lord" for any service to Him (Ephesians 6:7–8). Jesus stated that even as we serve our enemies — for whom we could never expect anything in return — God will see to it that even in this circumstance our reward will be great (Luke 6:35). Serving a righteous God assures us with the knowledge that our "toil is not in vain in the Lord" (1 Corinthians 15:58). Our righteous God is a "rewarder of those who seek Him" (Hebrews 11:6).

God will ultimately bless and favor the righteous man (Psalm 5:12). The deepest desires of the righteous are good (Proverbs 11:23) and will be granted (Proverbs 10:24). While each generation has to make their own decisions, blessing is promised to the descendants of the righteous (Proverbs 11:21; 20:7). The reward of true prosperity and honor (Proverbs

13:21; 21:21) will be clearly seen when the righteous are "repaid at the resurrection of the righteous" (Luke 14:14). One who may be overlooked, deprived, hated, and scorned will be remembered forever on that day and will experience his or her reward in heaven (Luke 6:20–23). One who lives righteously and who leads others to righteousness will be rewarded for all eternity (Daniel 12:3).

When We Suffer for Doing Right

Knowing that God will ultimately reward a believer for every work of faith motivated by love frees one to place a higher priority on pleasing God than pleasing man (Galatians 1:10). Even when our right responses bring suffering or ridicule, we know that this righteous God will ultimately vindicate us for all eternity. That reality also frees us from having to take our own personal revenge.

There have always been "enemies of righteousness" (cf. Acts 13:10) who speak arrogantly against righteous people (Psalm 31:18), who plot against them (Psalm 37:12), and spy upon and even seek to kill them (Psalm 37:32). There are those who may profit temporarily by lying and unrighteous deeds. However, "Truthful lips are only for a moment, but the truth will be established forever" (Proverbs 12:19).

For this reason, we are to refuse to take vengeance into our own hands (1 Samuel 26:23; Romans 12:19). Our unrighteous anger is not what achieves God's righteous vindication (James 1:20). Our supreme example is Christ, "who committed no sin, nor was any deceit found in His mouth; and while being reviled, He did not revile in return; while suffering, He uttered no threats, but kept entrusting Himself to Him who judges righteously" (1 Peter 2:22–23).

At the end of Paul's life, he referred to one who had done him much harm but also expressed the confidence that "the Lord will repay him according to his deeds" (2 Timothy 4:14). For that reason Peter also instructed Christians to not return "evil for evil or insult for insult, but giving a blessing instead; for you were called for the very purpose that you might inherit a blessing" (1 Peter 3:9).

The believer's safety and security are ultimately found in the name or character of our righteous God (Proverbs 12:3; 18:10). It is He who performs righteous deeds for the oppressed (Psalm 103:6) and ultimately condemns those who hate the righteous (Psalm 34:21). No real harm will befall the righteous (Proverbs 12:21) as God works all things together for our eternal good (Romans 8:28). He provides for us an everlasting foundation (Proverbs 10:25) and gives us the refuge of heavenly vindication when we die (cf. Proverbs 14:32).

In this life we will be *guarded* and *delivered* from anything that would hinder His righteous purposes for us being completed (Psalm 34:19). He will not forsake the righteous (Psalms 37:25; 55:22) but will sustain them (Psalm 37:17) and uphold them with His righteous right hand (Isaiah 41:10). The believer is to place his vindication into the hands of the righteous God whose eyes are toward the righteous and whose ears are open to their prayers (1 Peter 3:12). He promises to be with the righteous (Psalm 14:5), and "if God is for us, who is against us?" (Romans 8:31).

What God Provides
That We May Live Righteously

If righteous living doesn't come naturally, how can we live righteously? God provides resources that we may have power to live righteously. These resources begin with Christ and continue in the Holy Spirit.

1. *The gift of Christ's propitiation.* Christ's death has satisfied God's righteousness and freed the believer from God's condemning wrath (Romans 3:25). Prior to our salvation we were described as "children of wrath" (Ephesians 2:3), but now we are objects of His mercy, love, grace, and kindness (Ephesians 2:4–10).
2. *The gift of Christ's imputed righteousness.* Our righteous God requires perfect obedience to His moral law in order to be accepted by Him. Christ not only came to die to pay the penalty for our disobedience, but to credit His righteousness to the account of the believer (2 Corinthians 5:21).
3. *The gift of His regeneration.* His righteousness merits for us all of God's blessings (2 Peter 1:3–4). We are not saved by our righteousness (Titus 3:5). On the basis of His righteousness, our spirits have been graciously made alive or regenerated (Romans 8:10). We are now new creations (Ephesians 4:24) who are no longer slaves of sin but now slaves of righteousness (Romans 6:17–18).
4. *The gift of His Spirit.* Our righteous God has not only set us free from sin's control but also has given us the gift of the Holy Spirit. As one walks by the Spirit, the righteous requirements of God's eternal moral law are fulfilled in us (Romans 8:4).
5. *The gift of His leading.* The Lord loves righteousness (Psalm 11:7) and loves those who pursue righteousness (Proverbs 15:9). For this reason we can appeal to His righteousness to lead us (Psalm 5:8), to "bring [our souls] out of trouble" (Psalm 143:11), and even to revive

us (Psalm 119:40). We can appeal to His honor or name to lead us into paths where we can live righteously (Psalm 23:3).

6. *The gift of His cleansing.* Our righteous God does not desire us to sin. However, He has provided a way for the believer to walk with Him and be restored to fellowship when we do sin. As we walk in the light (1 John 1:7) and confess our sins as God points them out, He is not only faithful but also righteous in cleansing and forgiving us (1 John 1:9). In this way we are able to enjoy the fellowship of our righteous God who "knows the way of the righteous" (Psalm 1:6) and who will "meet [those] who [rejoice] in doing righteousness" (Isaiah 64:5).

God's Final Provision: His Discipline

Because He loves us and a father's love includes discipline (see Hebrews 12:7–11), *God's final provision is loving discipline.* Discipline is correction designed to yield the "peaceful fruit of righteousness" (v. 11). God disciplines His people by allowing them to experience the consequence of insisting upon their own way. When Israel disobeyed, God "gave them over to the stubbornness of their heart, to walk in their own devices" (Psalm 81:11–12).

Knowing Him

The Character of the Righteous

Together, Psalms and Proverbs reveal that the righteous man and woman demonstrate many noble character qualities. The righteous are

- teachable (Proverbs 9:9),
- compassionate (Proverbs 12:10),
- seekers of justice (Proverbs 29:7),
- gracious and giving (Psalm 37:21; Proverbs 21:26), and
- courageous like a lion (Proverbs 28:1).

God loves His people and desires good even for those who are under His discipline.

Oh that My people would listen to Me, that Israel would walk in My ways! I would quickly subdue their enemies and turn My hand against their adversaries. Those who hate the Lord would pretend obedience to Him, and their time of punishment would be forever. But I would feed you with the finest of the wheat, and with honey from the rock I would satisfy you. (Psalm 81:13–16)

God is open to the cry of the repentant and to those who intercede on their behalf (Daniel 9:16).

Descriptions of a
Life of Righteousness

There are many signs of righteous living. The righteous person seeks to live in light of his position as a new creation and a slave of righteousness (Romans 6:18). One's righteousness is to be displayed in a repentant lifestyle (Daniel 4:27) and in paying careful attention to God's revealed Word (Isaiah 48:18). We are to hunger and thirst for it (Matthew 5:6) as we make a decisive break with all lawlessness (2 Corinthians 6:14).

The righteous person is characterized as teachable (Proverbs 9:9), compassionate (Proverbs 12:10), hating falsehood (Proverbs 13:5), concerned for the rights of the poor (Proverbs 29:7), and as gracious and giving (Psalm 37:21; Proverbs 21:26). Her lips ponder how to answer (Proverbs 15:28), utter wisdom and speak justice (Psalm 37:30), feed many (Proverbs 10:21), promote life (Proverbs 10:11), delight kings (Proverbs 16:13), and give thanks to God (Psalm 140:13).

The righteous woman has learned to live by faith (Habakkuk 2:4) in her God who gives the gift of imputed righteousness (Romans 5:17) and enables her to live righteously (Romans 8:3-4). For this reason her life is characterized by effective prayer (James 5:16).

This life of faith also enables the righteous man and woman to rise every time they fall (Proverbs 24:16) and to be bold as a lion (Proverbs 28:1).

Righteousness Is the Key to Joy

Who was the most joyous person who ever lived? Hebrews tells us it is the One who "loved righteousness and hated lawlessness," Jesus Christ: "You have loved righteousness and hated lawlessness; therefore God, your God, has anointed You with the oil of gladness above Your companions" (Hebrews 1:9).

The idea of righteousness is to conform to a standard. Jesus, although called the Man of Sorrows, was the most joyous person who ever lived because He lived in perfect harmony with the Father.

Yet the righteous man and woman may also experience joy. Notice how the theme of joy and rejoicing are often linked with righteousness:

Be glad in the Lord and rejoice, you righteous ones; and shout for joy, all you who are upright in heart. (Psalm 32:11)

Sing for joy in the Lord, O you righteous ones; praise is becoming to the upright. (Psalm 33:1)

The righteous man will be glad in the Lord and will take refuge in Him; and all the upright in heart will glory. (Psalm 64:10)

Be glad in the Lord, you righteous ones, and give thanks to His holy name. (Psalm 97:12)

They shall eagerly utter the memory of Your abundant goodness and will shout joyfully of Your righteousness. (Psalm 145:7)

The righteous man has a joyful lot even when he has very little of the earth's treasures. He has learned that "better is a little with righteousness than great income with injustice" (Proverbs 16:8). Jesus even instructed the righteous to rejoice when they are persecuted and insulted.

> Blessed are those who have been persecuted for the sake of righteousness, for theirs is the kingdom of heaven.
> Blessed are you when people insult you and persecute you, and falsely say all kinds of evil against you because of Me. Rejoice and be glad, for your reward in heaven is great; for in the same way they persecuted the prophets who were before you. (Matthew 5:10–12)

The Future Day of Righteousness

The believer in Christ has been declared righteous — "justified" (Romans 5:1) — but also has the hope of righteousness (Galatians 5:5). One day "we will be like Him, because we will see Him just as He is" (1 John 3:2). This is our hope of glorification, which is the final phase of God's great plan of salvation: foreknowledge, predestination, calling, justification, and glorification (Romans 8:29–30).

When Israel rejected God as their Ruler, He disciplined them by allowing them to experience the rule of wicked Assyria and Babylon. Today those who refuse to live under the control of the Spirit, He disciplines by letting them be ruled by their own self-will. This is not freedom but discipline! However, one day the promise that the "scepter of wickedness shall not rest upon the land of the righteous" (Psalm 125:3) will be ultimately fulfilled in the future kingdom.

A godly ruler is one who, like David, administers justice and righteousness for all the people (2 Samuel 8:15). This is certainly to be our prayer for all in authority (1 Timothy 2:1–2).

It will be fulfilled in a perfect sense by the greater David, the son of David—the Messiah. His throne will be established and upheld with justice and righteousness (Isaiah 9:7). He will judge and rule every matter with righteousness (Isaiah 11:4) and is even referred to as the righteous Branch (Jeremiah 23:5; 33:15–16).

In this future day "everlasting righteousness" will be ushered in (Daniel 9:24). As the sun sends its rays everywhere, so the display of righteousness throughout the earth is referred to as the "sun of righteousness" rising with "healing in its wings" (Malachi 4:2). It will be a time of fertility, peace, quietness, and confidence (Isaiah 32:16–17). There will be no more oppression or cause for fear (Isaiah 54:14), and "the Lord God will cause righteousness and praise to spring up before all the nations" (Isaiah 61:11).

The eternal state is referred to as the day of God (2 Peter 3:12). After the destruction of the present heavens and earth, there will be "new heavens and a new earth, in which righteousness dwells" (2 Peter 3:13)! Our righteous God will fully triumph and usher in for His people a perfect environment of righteousness and joy for all eternity.

Note

1. For more discussion on how to enjoy this continual cleansing, see Bill Thrasher, *How to Be a Soul Physician* (Seattle: CreateSpace, 2010), 211–34.

13

God Is Faithful and True

HE ALONE IS ABSOLUTELY TRUSTWORTHY

GOD IS DESCRIBED as the "only true God" (John 17:3). Faithfulness surrounds Him (Psalm 89:8) and reaches to every part of His creation (Psalm 36:5). When His people abandoned Him for idols, they were still religious, but they were "without the true God" (2 Chronicles 15:3).

God is true in that He is consistent with Himself, the source of all truth, and perfectly reliable in all His dealings with His creation. He plans with perfect faithfulness (Isaiah 25:1) and all His work is done in faithfulness (Psalm 33:4) — even His judgment (Psalms 54:5; 96:13).

The Teller of Truth Versus the Teller of Lies

God is the truth teller. His Word is absolutely reliable. In contrast, men and women regularly hear the lies of God's adversary — an angelic creature whose most common names are the "Devil" and "Satan." Jesus has characterized Satan as "a liar and the father of lies," adding, "There is no truth in him" (John 8:44). In contrast, God is characterized as a faithful and true God who *cannot* lie (Hebrews 6:18; Titus 1:2). It is for this reason that we are told to put on the belt of truth (Ephesians 6:14) as a piece of our armor in our spiritual battles.

Cursed is the person who places his ultimate confidence in people (Jeremiah 17:5–6). For a variety of reasons, people are not always faithful. It may be because of fear, the distraction of some outside influence, or even a lack of desire or interest in remaining faithful. In contrast to this is a God who says, "[I will not] deal falsely in My faithfulness" (Psalm 89:33). Those who trust in Him will never be ultimately disappointed (Romans 9:33; 10:11) but will be blessed (Jeremiah 17:7–8).

His Word and Promises Can Be Trusted

If God were not completely faithful, a revelation from Him would be a mockery. Would it really matter what He said if we could not be absolutely confident that His Word is always reliable? Yet Joshua could declare with utmost confidence what he had beheld as he brought the people into the Promised Land and secured it against Israel's enemies: "Not one of the good promises which the Lord had made to the house of Israel failed; all came to pass" (Joshua 21:45).

Since "He who promised is faithful" (Hebrews 10:23), are you expecting Him to do all that He has promised? Believe God to teach you His Word in a way that you can understand it, personalize it, and stake your life on it.

Lean on God's Faithfulness . . .

Because God is faithful, we can rely on His promises in all times, both good and bad. In key times, God will not abandon us. Consider these special times when God is there to sustain us.

. . . When He Offers His Salvation

It is the faithful God who calls one into fellowship with Himself through the gospel (1 Corinthians 1:9). It is for us to respond in faith to this sovereign and gracious call. If we do, He accepts us, just as He says (John 1:12).

The first stage of the Jewish wedding is a betrothal or binding engagement. This imagery is used to give us a picture of our relationship with God. For this reason Scripture speaks of Israel being betrothed in *faithfulness* (Hosea 2:20). The New Testament believer is also betrothed to Christ (2 Corinthians 11:2). We are not only to respond in faith to the initial call for salvation but also to be faithful to our faithful God throughout our relationship with Him. Sin is grievous because it is an act of unfaithfulness against an absolutely faithful God. Lean on His faithfulness to maintain the relationship that He initiated.

. . . At the Beginning of Each Day

Why is it sometimes hard to get up in the morning? It may not only be due to physical tiredness. It has often been said that many strong men are pinned by the sheets each morning. Is it not sometimes because there may be something that we do not want to face that day? As long as we stay under the sheets, we do not have to face it.

What can give us the courage to get out of bed and face the day with confidence? It is the realization that we will be met by the faithfulness of God. His compassions are "new every morning" because His faithfulness is great (Lamentations 3:23)! Let your first thought each day be that you will be met by a fresh manifestation of God's faithful, compassionate help.

The beginning of a day is the rudder of that day. It sets the tone for the day. For this reason the psalmist told the Lord that each morning He would hear his voice as he ordered his prayer to God and eagerly anticipated God's answer (Psalm 5:3). Our prayer to God is best seen as only a response to hearing His loving-kindness expressed to us each morning (Psalm 143:8).

Romans 15:5 is the verse that got me out of bed every morning during a difficult time. In this verse God promises to give us encouragement and endurance. Let your first thoughts each day be a response and anticipation of being met by a faithful God.

. . . At the End of Each Day

Each evening is also a time to declare God's faithfulness (Psalm 92:2). Take time to review each day in light of God's faithful compassion to you. As you relive His kind gifts to you, you will experience the joy of these afresh and thanksgiving will fill your heart.

. . . During Trials and Temptations

Our times of temptation are a time to experience the faithfulness of God, according to 1 Corinthians 10:13: "No temptation has overtaken you but such as is common to man; and *God is faithful*, who will not allow you to be tempted beyond what you are able, but with the temptation will provide the way of escape also, so that you will be able to endure it" (italics added).

How can you lean on God's faithfulness during such times? Lean on His faithfulness to give you hope in your trials and temptations and to use the shield of faith to knock down the fiery darts of despair that will be thrown at you (see Ephesians 6:16). Lean on His faithfulness to prepare you for every trial and temptation that is coming. Sometimes this preparation will be your obedience to the command of Romans 13:14—to make no provision for your fleshly desires. You cannot play with sin and have victory over it. At other times His preparation may be not telling you what is ahead to prevent you from having a spirit of dread in your life.

When the trial comes, God's grace will be sufficient, and you can then discern the blessing your faithful God has for you. Depend on your faithful God to meet you in your temptation and trial with His merciful and gracious aid (Hebrews 4:16). These are special times to experience His faithfulness.

. . . During Times of Satanic Conflict

Paul declares God's faithfulness in speaking of His work of guarding the believer from the Evil One and strengthening him (2 Thessalonians 3:3). Our spiritual battles often arise by the temptations of Satan (Ephesians 6:12–13). To be sure, we are fully capable of sinning against God without the Devil's help, but he can tempt us and intensify the efforts of our flesh as he sows his lies for us to believe.

We need to lean upon God's faithfulness in exposing Satan's schemes against us personally, for we are not to be ignorant of his schemes (2 Corinthians 2:11). We can also lean on His faithfulness to aid us in appropriating God's provisions to stand firm in our spiritual battle. We are to depend on His strength (Ephesians 6:10–11) and the armor that He has provided (Ephesians 6:13–17). The believer has a wicked enemy but also a faithful God who will protect us and strengthen us in this battle! His faithfulness is our shield (Psalm 91:4)!

. . . During Times of Suffering

Peter instructs the suffering believers to "entrust their souls to a faithful Creator in doing what is right" (1 Peter 4:19). How do you lean on God's faithfulness during times of suffering? First of all, lean on God's faithfulness to give you any needed insight into the reason of the suffering. It is possible to bring suffering on ourselves due to a violation of God's principles. In other words, suffering may be due to our personal sin. If so, God will faithfully convict us and give us opportunity to restore ourselves to Him. He will be working together for good, even the mess we created! He will not abandon us; He is faithful.

On other occasions suffering may come so that we may rely on Him, to draw us closer to Him, or to strengthen our faith and thus bring Him glory in our responses before others (2 Corinthians 1:8–9; 12:9–10).

Believers will also look to their faithful God to help them put the suffering in perspective of eternity. A sense of perspective can be a relief to our soul. The trial will not last forever.

Knowing Him

That Eternal Perspective

Whether you're facing trials, temptations, or a time of suffering, having that eternal perspective gives you hope and even confidence in the present situation. Two godly followers of Christ, Peter and Paul, each found a focus on the future helpful to themselves and the believers they knew.

Paul, in the midst of his suffering, wrote, "I consider that the sufferings of this present time are not worthy to be compared with the glory that is to be revealed to us" (Romans 8:18).

Peter wrote to fellow believers, "In this you greatly rejoice, even though now for a little while, if necessary, you have been distressed by various trials, so that the proof of your faith, being more precious than gold which is perishable, even though tested by fire, may be found to result in praise and glory and honor at the revelation of Jesus Christ" (1 Peter 1:6–7).

Believers can also look to their faithful God to use the trial for their good. The psalmist declared that in God's faithfulness he was afflicted (Psalm 119:75). We can trust God to use it for our eternal good and to communicate to us any insight we need to know in regard to the trial. We can also trust Him to vindicate us when we suffer for doing what is right, for the Messiah's mission is to faithfully bring about justice (Isaiah 42:3).

. . . When You Are in
Need of Cleansing and Restoration

When we sin, we are sinning against a God who is absolutely faithful to us (Hosea 11:12)! He is not only faithful to convict us but also faithful to forgive us and cleanse as we confess our sins to Him. The Bible promises that when "we confess our sins, He is *faithful* and righteous to forgive us our sins and to cleanse us from all unrighteousness" (1 John 1:9, italics added).

. . . In Your Thinking about the Future

Paul speaks of our ultimate sanctification in 1 Thessalonians 5:23: "Now may the God of peace Himself sanctify you entirely; and may your spirit and soul and body be preserved complete, without blame at the coming of our Lord Jesus Christ."

Imagine being like Him in our desire and our movement toward holiness. Sanctification is becoming like Christ in our thoughts, desires, and service toward others (John 13:13–17). We are promised that one day we will be wholly set apart for God and like Him. The security of this future accomplishment rests on the faithfulness of God: "Faithful is He who calls you, and He also will bring it to pass" (1 Thessalonians 5:24).

Christ told His followers to not be anxious for the tomorrows of their lives (Matthew 6:34). When we are tempted to be anxious, remember the faithfulness of God that will meet us afresh every morning (Lamentations 3:23).

. . . In the Completion of Any Task

At one point in my life, I had my prayer life divided up into different categories for each day. On Thursday I prayed for all the various "tasks" in which I was presently working. I put Psalm 37:5 at the top of that prayer list: "Commit your way to the Lord, trust also in Him, and He will do it" (Psalm 37:5).

As I prayed, I would ask myself, *What am I doing that I am not doing with trust in the Lord? Have I committed the task to the Lord?* You cannot trust God with anything that you have not committed to Him. *Am I trusting Him with this task?* I would ask myself. As you trust Him, God will show you what you are to do. He will also accomplish what concerns you.

King David wrote with confidence in Psalm 138: "The Lord will accomplish what concerns me; Your lovingkindness, O Lord, is everlasting; do not forsake the works of Your hands" (v. 8).

God uses those who have learned to put all their concerns—the small ones and the large ones—into His hands moment by moment. Do not be overly concerned about your influence. Depend upon your faithful God day by day—committing every detail to Him, trusting Him, and watching Him work.

The Standard of Faithfulness

As we look to our faithful God, He will transform us into faithful people. The sad commentary is that it is rare to find a trustworthy person. "Many a man proclaims his own loyalty, but who can find a trustworthy man?" (Proverbs 20:6). The psalmist also speaks of the faithful "disappearing from

among the sons of men" (Psalm 12:1) and of how past generations of God's people were not faithful to God in their
spirits (Psalm 78:8).

The person who is faithful will find favor and have a
good reputation in the eyes of God and man (Proverbs 3:3–
4). The key to being faithful is being faithful in the little things
of life (Luke 16:10). Those who are faithful in the use of the
money God has entrusted to them will also be given true
eternal riches (Luke 16:11). If we are faithful in the use of
another person's resources, God will entrust us with those of
our own (Luke 16:12).

As the believer opens His life to the control of God's
Spirit, He will work the fruit of faithfulness in us (Galatians
5:22). The faithful person will "abound with blessings"
(Proverbs 28:20), and God delights in those who deal faithfully (Proverbs 12:22).

The Standard of Truthfulness

Lying and cheating have become an acceptable norm
among many. According to one survey a few years ago, over
90 percent of college students said they would cheat to get a job.[1]

Becoming a Christian means one has been delivered from
Satan's kingdom of darkness and lives in Christ's kingdom.
His kingdom is characterized by truth.

When a businessman came up to me and told me that his
boss did not expect him to always be truthful, I took him to
these Proverbs:

There are six things which the Lord hates, yes, seven
which are an abomination to Him: Haughty eyes, a lying

tongue . . . a false witness who utters lies, and one who spreads strife among brothers. (Proverbs 6:16–17a, 19)

Truthful lips will be established forever, but a lying tongue is only for a moment. (12:19)

Lying lips are an abomination to the Lord, but those who deal faithfully are His delight. (12:22)

A false witness will not go unpunished, and he who tells lies will not escape. (19:5)

Bread obtained by falsehood is sweet to a man, but afterward his mouth will be filled with gravel. (20:17)

The acquisition of treasures by a lying tongue is a fleeting vapor, the pursuit of death. (21:6)

A false witness will perish, but the man who listens to the truth will speak forever. (21:28)

The eyes of the Lord preserve knowledge, but He overthrows the words of the treacherous man. (22:12)

The businessman walked away with the commitment to be a truthful man.

Obey the Holy Spirit as you consider the following questions:

1. Have you corrected the lies that you have told in the past and asked forgiveness for them?

2. Do you tend to exaggerate the facts in order to gain the approval of others?
3. Have you made right any previous cheating?
4. Do you tell God the precise sins you commit and claim His forgiveness?

Place of Trust

We would despair if we placed our ultimate confidence in ourselves or in any other human. Only God can give us the promise that if we trust in Him, we will never be ultimately disappointed (Romans 10:11). Even when we are faithless, He remains faithful (2 Timothy 2:13). He not only is faithful to forgive our sins (1 John 1:9) but also can heal our faithlessness (cf. Jeremiah 3:22). Our unbelief and lying cannot change the truth that He is always and absolutely a faithful and true God (Romans 3:3–4).

Our faithful God is able to guard what we entrust to Him (2 Timothy 1:12)! Give Him your life, your reputation, and all your concerns. Remember that He is faithful to all generations (Psalms 100:5; 119:90).

God tells His people Israel that He has taken care of them from birth and carried them from the womb. He also promises to be the same even to their old age and graying years. Look at Isaiah 46:3–4!

You can be secure in trusting a faithful God. Purpose to declare His faithfulness (Psalm 30:9), speak of it often (Psalm 40:9), make it known every chance that you can (Psalm 89:1), declare it every night that you review your days (Psalm 92:2), and tell it to your children (Isaiah 38:19). We worship a faithful God!

Note

1. "Spiritual Shortcuts," *Christianity Today*, January 2005, 27.

14

God Is Love
HE WANTS YOU TO EXPERIENCE HIS LOVE

a FRIEND SENT ME by e-mail a list of definitions he found on the Internet given by children who were asked to complete the sentence "Love is . . ." Here are some of their definitions of love. "Love is . . .

- when you tell someone something bad about yourself and you're scared they won't love you anymore. But then you get surprised because not only do they still love you, they love you even more."
  — MATTHEW, age seven
- when my grandmother got arthritis, she couldn't bend over and paint her toenails anymore. So my grandfather does it for her all the time, even when his hands got arthritis too. That's love." — REBECCA, age eight

- when you go out to eat and give somebody most of your French fries without making them give you any of theirs."   —CHRISSY, age six
- what's in the room with you at Christmas if you stop opening presents and listen."   —BOBBY, age seven
- when you tell a guy you like his shirt, then he wears it every day."   —NOELLE, age seven
- like a little old woman and a little old man who are still friends even after they know each other so well."
                                               —TOMMY, age six
- During my piano recital, I was on a stage and I was scared. I looked at all the people watching me and saw my daddy waving and smiling. He was the only one doing that. I wasn't scared anymore."
                                               —CINDY, age eight
- when Mommy gives Daddy the best piece of chicken."
                                               —ELAINE, age five
- when Mommy sees Daddy smelly and sweaty and still says he is handsomer than Robert Redford."
                                               —CHRIS, age seven
- when your puppy licks your face even after you left him alone all day."   —MARY ANN, age four[1]

The Source of
Genuine, Unfailing Love

While these comments hint at the nature of love, we must turn to the Scriptures to truly understand love. True love is found in and expressed by God. Two great verses in John's first epistle declare that truth:

Beloved, let us love one another, for *love is from God;* and everyone who loves is born of God and knows God. (1 John 4:7, all italics added)

We have come to know and have believed the love which God has for us. *God is love,* and the one who abides in love abides in God, and God abides in him. (1 John 4:16)

God is careful to tell us that His love is more faithful and more compassionate than even a mother's love for her nursing baby.

> But Zion said, "The Lord has forsaken me, and the Lord has forgotten me."
> "Can a woman forget her nursing child and have no compassion on the son of her womb? Even these may forget, but I will not forget you. Behold, I have inscribed you on the palms of My hands; your walls are continually before Me." (Isaiah 49:14–16)

The Bible depicts love in a poignant way in Genesis after God instructs Abraham to obey an unusual request: "Take now your son, your only son, whom you love, Isaac, and go to the land of Moriah and offer him there as a burnt offering on one of the mountains of which I will tell you" (Genesis 22:2).

This verse tells us of a father's love and delight in a son. It also prepares us to learn of our loving heavenly Father who demonstrated His love by sacrificing His beloved Son for us in our need. He has not only spoken of His love but has "manifested" it to us and demonstrated it by sending His Son to bear the punishment of our sin that we deserved.

In this is love, not that we loved God, but that He loved us and sent His Son to be the propitiation for our sins. (1 John 4:10)

We know love by this, that [Christ] laid down His life for us; and we ought to lay down our lives for the brethren. (1 John 3:16)

He is not only the source of all love — "Love is from God" (1 John 4:7) — but His very essence is described as love — "God is love" (1 John 4:8, 16).

God's Love in Relation to His Other Attributes

God's love is the attribute that manifests itself in His desire and delight in His creation, the provision of personal fellowship with Himself, and His joy in giving of His Son for our eternal benefit. The apostle Paul fittingly described this attribute as a "great love" (Ephesians 2:4).

If it is correctly understood, you can never overestimate God's love. His other attributes help us to understand it.

- *His love is eternal.* It is called everlasting in Jeremiah 31:3.
- *His love is infinite.* Note how God's love is personalized in Galatians 2:20, as Paul describes the Father as the one "who loved *me*." Because God has no limits, He can love you as if you were the only person in the world and not take His attention away from anyone else.
- *His love is holy.* "For those whom the Lord loves He disciplines" (Hebrews 12:6), and He does so "for our

good, so that we may share His holiness" (Hebrews
12:10; see also Revelation 3:19).
- *His love is faithful.* You can know and trust the love that
  God has for us (1 John 4:16) because you cannot be
  separated from it (Romans 8:38–39) and He will love
  us "to the end" (John 13:1).
- *His love is sovereign.* On the basis of His love, He chooses
  (Deuteronomy 4:37), appoints authority (2 Chronicles
  2:11), and even overrules what people mean for curses
  and turns them into blessings (Deuteronomy 23:5).
- *His love is righteous.* It is a righteous love because He is
  righteous and loves righteousness (Psalm 11:7).
- *His love is gracious.* It is a gracious love as He even loves
  us in our sin (Hosea 3:1; Romans 5:8).

You cannot overemphasize love if it is correctly understood.

Love: The Most Important Thing

Love is the primary thing, and without it nothing else
has any eternal value. One can have an amazing ability to
communicate, but without love we are only producing an
unpleasant sound. You can give sacrificially to help the poor,
but if your action is not motivated by love, there is no eternal profit (1 Corinthians 13:1–3). It is for this reason that we
live under the command to "let all that you do be done in
love" (1 Corinthians 16:14).

We are told to pursue love (1 Corinthians 14:1) and to seek
to stimulate each other to live lives of love (Hebrews 10:24).

Why is this the most important thing you can trust
God for? Because the Scriptures say that love is the most

important thing, and without it everything else is worthless (1 Corinthians 13:1–3). The Scriptures also state that
our love is only a response to His love for us: "We love,
because He first loved us" (1 John 4:19). In light of these
two truths, the most important thing that you and I can ask
God for is to overwhelm us with His love so that we can
better respond in loving Him and loving others.

At Jesus' baptism He heard the Father's words: "This is
My beloved Son, in whom I am well pleased" (Matthew 3:17).
God wants to say this to your heart and to my heart. You
might respond, "Yes, but this verse is referring to Jesus." Let
me remind you of Jesus' prayer in John 17:23. He prayed
that God's people would experience a true spiritual unity so
the world might know that the Father had sent Him and that
the Father loves His children with the same intensity as His
own Son! We all need to pray this truth into our lives.

Ask God to Overwhelm
You with His Love

The first step in the pursuit of love is to come to the "God
of love and peace" (2 Corinthians 13:11) and trust Him to
overwhelm you with His love for you. You must realize that
there is a difference between knowing the fact that God loves
you and letting this truth "control" your life (2 Corinthians
5:14). There is a difference in knowing a truth and "treasur-
ing" that truth within you (Proverbs 7:1) so that it "abides in
you" (John 15:7).

God wants you to be more certain of His love for you
than anything else, for nothing is more foundational. He
delights in you and desires to be with you. God is pictured
as rejoicing over His people (Zephaniah 3:17). Remember

that our Lord told His disciples how much He loved them (John 15:9), even though He knew they would fail Him that very night! This did not stop Him from giving His life for them. This is a love that "surpasses knowledge" (Ephesians 3:19)!

Experiencing the Answer to Your Prayers

We begin this pursuit of love in our prayers. One year I asked God to overwhelm me with His love so I might better love Him and the people around me. Later that year God opened up familiar passages to me in a way I have never seen them before. To be sure, I "knew" them and could even quote some of them from memory. However, when I began to digest very familiar passages such as Romans 5:5–10, my life began to change. Whom did God set His love upon?

- *The helpless* (v. 6). I asked myself — and you should ask yourself — *When I am weak, sick, and powerless, do I sense His love?*
- *The ungodly* (v. 6). One summer day that year, I felt particularly ungodly. However, I sensed God's love for me in a way I had never known before.
- *Sinners* (v. 8). I realized this is not only a verse to share with the spiritually lost. It is also a verse for God's children to experience daily. Remember that the person who realizes how much he or she has been forgiven is the one who "loves much" (Luke 7:47). Just one wrong thought is enough for a holy God to sentence you to hell forever and be perfectly just for doing so. We have been forgiven much.

• *His enemies* (v. 10). Now that we are His reconciled friends, do we try to perform for His love or do we rest in it and let it transform us?

A Personal Pursuit

Romans 5:5–10 compares God's love to the best of men who might even die for a good man. However, God is viewed as being better than the best of men. You are not experiencing His love as He would desire you to until you see that He loves you in a way that no one else ever will or can.

As I prayed this prayer that God would overwhelm me with His love, I looked at His commands for me to love in a new way. For example, let's take the truth of Proverbs 17:9. "He who conceals a transgression seeks love, but he who repeats a matter separates intimate friends."

As I studied this verse, I reviewed once more how God had first loved me so that I might know how He was asking me to love another. Remember, "We love, because He first loved us" (1 John 4:19). His command for me to forgive and not repeatedly bring up another's faults reflects His approach; this is how He deals with me as His child. What if you got up each morning and He rubbed all your past sins in your face? He does not do so because He is seeking to build a relationship of love (cf. Ephesians 5:1–2).

Let's follow this line of thinking with another verse, Proverbs 17:17: "A friend loves at all times, and a brother is born for adversity."

In approaching this verse, I would first of all praise God that He is that kind of faithful support to me. I would then ask Him for the grace to be that to others. I have pages of notes from trusting God with this prayer, which are very precious to me. May God do even more for you as you trust Him to overwhelm you with His love! Here are a few of the notations on one of my pages, reminders to me (and you) of how God is available, like a brother—but a perfect brother—to show His love.

- He is one who is available to you anytime you humbly come to Him.
- He does not belittle you but even looks forward to your coming to Him as if you were the most important person in the world.
- He is always thinking of you.
- His love alone is totally pure toward you because He does not come to you with any lack in His life.
- He cares about every detail of your life and this care extends to every moment of your life.
- His love is based on a perfect understanding of you that enables you to fully develop as a person.

To my understanding there is only one place in the New Testament where the present tense of love is used in relationship to God. It is most often used in the past tense—"For God so *loved* the world" (John 3:16). Of course, because He is unchanging, His love is also a present reality. However, the one place that it is used in the present tense is in Revelation 1:5.

And from Jesus Christ, the faithful witness, the firstborn of the dead, and the ruler of the kings of the earth. To Him who *loves* us and released us from our sins by His blood. (Revelation 1:5, italics added)

Note how this passage teaches us that the Ruler of the kings of the earth *loves* us! May God "direct your [heart] into the love of God" (2 Thessalonians 3:5) as you trust Him to overwhelm you with His love.

Knowing God's Love Personally

How can we know God loves us? Romans 5:5–8 gives us two lines of evidence. First, there is the external, historical evidence. There is the historical fact that Christ came to earth and died for sin, and this was done as a demonstration of His love (Romans 5:8). However, there are people who know this historical fact and yet are not controlled by the truth that God loves them. There is also the subjective, internal witness of the Spirit that is referred to in Romans 5:5: "And hope does not disappoint, because the love of God has been poured out within our hearts through the Holy Spirit who was given to us."

We need God's Spirit to witness to us and assure us of this truth that at one level we already know (cf. Romans 8:16). You need to internalize this historical truth for yourself so that you can say with Paul, "I am trusting the Lord who loved me and delivered Himself up for me" (see Galatians 2:20).

As you open your life up for the Spirit to let Christ "dwell in your hearts" (Ephesians 3:17), you are able to comprehend and experience all of the dimensions of Christ's love for you (Ephesians 3:18–19). Jesus spoke of how the one who has and keeps His commandments would be loved by God (John 14:21, 23).

When Jesus states that God loves the obedient believer, is He making God's love conditional? No! He set His love upon us when we were helpless, ungodly sinners, and His enemies. However, while a parent loves a disobedient child as well as the obedient child, which one will experience more of the parent's love? The obvious answer is the child who allows the parent to love him. It is for this reason that God tells us to open our lives to His Spirit so that Christ can dwell — control — our lives (Ephesians 3:16–19).

One student wrote to me about how their family had adopted a nine-year-old girl. Born with a cleft palate and cerebral palsy, the girl had been cruelly abused and neglected by her birth family. At the time of her adoption, her body had several large bruises from the beatings she had received. She was rarely bathed and covered with lice. Her buttocks were raw as she grew up without her diapers being regularly changed. She also was severely malnourished and weighed thirty-six pounds at age nine. This girl hated to be touched. In fact, she would shield herself from expected blows.

Ciara was a nonambulatory, angry, and fearful child who required twenty-four-hour care. Would she let her adoptive parents love her?

One night when Ciara was crying — the nights were particularly hard — her adoptive mother held her in her arms and began to cry over her. When Ciara felt this warm tear fall on her face, she seemed shocked to sense that someone cared for her and loved her. This was the beginning of her feeling free to open up her life to her new loving adopted family.

The love of Christ as exhibited by the Danielson family transformed Ciara's life. Of course, God used Ciara's life as an instrument to also transform their lives.

Asking you to open up your life completely to God may seem as scary as asking you to jump off a twenty-story building. However, you would do it if you knew it

was also opening yourself up to a God of love who promised to be right there to catch you!

> To love at all is to be vulnerable. Love anything and your
> heart will certainly be wrung and possibly broken. If you
> want to make sure of keeping it intact, you must give
> your heart to no one, not even to an animal. Wrap it care-
> fully around with hobbies and little luxuries . . . lock it up
> safe in the casket or coffin of your selfishness. But in that
> casket — safe, dark, motionless, airless — it will change. It
> will not be broken; it will become unbreakable, impene-
> trable, irredeemable. . . . The only place outside heaven
> where you can be perfectly safe from all the dangers of
> love is hell![1]

Beware of Competing Loves

In your pursuit of God's love, you need to be aware of
competing loves to making God and His Son Jesus your first
love.

First, there is a love for this world. In a famous passage, the
apostle John warns "not [to] love the world nor the things in
the world" (see 1 John 2:15–17). The "world" is a spiritual
system that is under the head of Satan (2 Corinthians 4:4). It
promotes a way of life independent of God. His appeals are
to the lusts of our flesh and our eyes and the pride of life
itself.[2]

Second, there is the love of possessions. As Paul warned
young Timothy, he warns us: "The love of money is a root of
all sorts of evil, and some by longing for it have wandered
away from the faith and pierced themselves with many

griefs" (1 Timothy 6:10). God tells us that we cannot love Him and love money (Matthew 6:24).

Third, there is the love of pleasure. Think about what the Bible teaches us about pleasures: The best things in life revolve around the Lord (Proverbs 15:16–17), and God is not a kill-joy but "richly supplies us with all things to enjoy" (1 Timothy 6:17).

Knowing Him

The Competing Love Called Pleasure

Of the many loves that compete to dethrone our love of God, none seems more innocent or less threatening than the love of pleasure. But compared to the riches of God's good riches, it is a meager counterfeit. The Proverbs often warn us to abandon fleeting pleasures for that which lasts. For example,

> Better is a little with the fear of the Lord than great treasure and turmoil with it. Better is a dish of vegetables where love is than a fattened ox served with hatred. (Proverbs 15:16–17)

> Do not love sleep, or you will become poor; open your eyes, and you will be satisfied with food. (Proverbs 20:13)

> He who loves pleasure will become a poor man; he who loves wine and oil will not become rich. (Proverbs 21:17)

Fourth, there is the love of people. We are to love others, and especially our family, but no person should be more important than our Lord. Jesus explained that the one "who loves father or mother more than Me is not worthy of Me; and he who loves son or daughter more than Me is not worthy of Me" (Matthew 10:37). As you love Christ supremely, your love for others will be purified and deepened. When we make an idol of a person, we destroy the experience of true love.

Fifth, there is the love of self. We must put His plans first, above our own wants and desires. Jesus told us that only after one decisively chooses to love his Lord supremely and lose his life will he truly experience the abundant life that Christ came to provide (John 10:10).

Embrace Christ as Your First Love

Those in the church of Ephesus are commended for their perseverance, labor, and intolerance of evil men and false teachers, but they are rebuked for leaving their first love (Revelation 2:2–4). What does it mean for Christ to be your first love, and that you have renounced a competing love?

- *Supreme loyalty to Christ.* Your love for the Lord will be tested when you are tempted to serve other gods (see Deuteronomy 13:2–3). Jesus explained that loving Him is having and keeping His commandments (John 14:15).
- *Preoccupation with Christ's desires.* Jesus modeled the abiding life by His preoccupation with the Father's desires and "always [doing] the things that are pleasing to Him" (John 8:29). So the major preoccupation of the believer in Christ is to be what Christ desires, even if pleasing Him brings you the displeasure of others (Galatians 1:10).

- *Hating evil.* The love for what is good is also accompanied by a hatred of that which opposes it (Psalm 97:10).

Conversely there are several signs that one has left their first love:

- *Not loving Christ's appearing* (2 Timothy 4:8). The three stages of the Jewish marriage were a betrothal or a binding engagement; secondly, the groom coming to claim his bride and take her to his home; and thirdly, a marriage feast or celebration that followed (Revelation 19:5). The believer in Christ is said to now be betrothed to Christ (2 Corinthians 11:2). We now await our Lord's return to earth to claim us as His bride and take us to heaven (John 14:1–3). It would be unthinkable to be engaged and never think of your wedding day! This would be a symptom that something is certainly wrong with your love relationship! Do you love Christ's appearing?
- *Fear of losing something or someone.* If you have an obsessive fear of losing something or someone and cannot trust God with this fear, this thing or person that you fear losing is probably your first love. Once Jesus spoke to a group of people who were preoccupied with seeking glory from men. For that reason the love of God was not in them, He said, and that was why they could not believe God (John 5:42, 44). Their fear of losing the approval of others caused them to neglect God's love.
- *Sensing His commandments are burdensome.* If you find His commandments to be burdensome, you may have left your first love (cf. 1 John 5:3).
- *Preoccupation with other things.* Where does your mind

go when you have leisure time? Where it usually goes is likely the direction of your first love.

How to Return to Your First Love

Our Lord does not point out a problem without also pointing us to a solution. He tells us in Revelation 2:5 to

- *Remember.* Remember that our relationship with God started when our mouths were shut (Romans 3:19). We realized our total need and dependence on our Savior to rescue us from our lost condition.
- *Repent.* Repent of any idol in your life. An idol is that which we are looking to in order to meet the thirst of our heart.
- *Repeat.* Do the deeds that you did at first. Just as you began the Christian life in total dependence on Christ for your salvation, so look to Him now for every spiritual, emotional, and physical need in your life each moment of each day. As Paul wrote, "Therefore as you have received Christ Jesus the Lord, so walk in Him" (Colossians 2:6).

The Fruit of Having Christ as Your First Love

There are many fruit to keeping Christ as your first love. Here are three key outcomes:

1. Confidence during trying times. We can be more than a conqueror in our trials "through Him who loved us"

(Romans 8:37). You can make it through anything if someone understands you, loves you, and is with you, caring for your eternal good.

2. Trust in God's timing. People had waited for the Messiah for many years but He came in the fullness of time (Galatians 4:4) and died at the right time (Romans 5:6). Notice what John 11:3–6 teaches us about trusting God's timing: If you know that Christ loves you (v. 5), you can trust His timing even when it seems He is doing nothing (v. 6)! You do not get upset at Jesus' action in this passage because you know the end of the story.[3] As you wait on your loving God today, trust His timing and purposes even when it seems He is not in a hurry.

3. Ability to face unhealthy fears.[4] You will never know that God loves you as He desires you to until you experience His helping you understand and process your fears (1 John 4:18).

Confident in His Love

A healthy love relationship with God the Father and God the Son will give you a confidence before God (1 John 3:18–22) and a confidence as you anticipate Christ's coming again and evaluating your life for the purpose of rewarding you (1 John 2:28; 4:17).

We can be confident because of the amazing promises the Scriptures give to those who love Him:

And we know that God causes all things to work together for good to those who love God, to those who are called according to His purpose. (Romans 8:28)

Things which eye has not seen and ear has not heard, and which have not entered the heart of man, all that God has prepared for those who love Him. (1 Corinthians 2:9)

Blessed is a man who perseveres under trial; for once he has been approved, he will receive the crown of life which the Lord has promised to those who love Him. (James 1:12)

Listen, my beloved brethren: did not God choose the poor of this world to be rich in faith and heirs of the kingdom which He promised to those who love Him? (James 2:5)

God is love! We love because He first loved us. We are not saved by the love we exercise but rather by the love we trust. It all begins with God and ends with His glory.

Notes

1. C. S. Lewis, *The Four Loves* (Orlando: Harcourt Brace, 1960), 169. For additional help in digesting God's loving acceptance, see Bill Thrasher, *How to Be a Soul Physician* (Seattle: CreateSpace, 2010), 25–96.

2. In 1 John 2:16, "The lust of the flesh" appeals to our urges; "the lust of the eyes" appeals to what looks attractive to us; and "the boastful pride of life" appeals to our selfish desires to exalt ourselves. Our loving God tells us to delight in Him and let Him give us the true desires of our heart (Psalm 37:4).

3. In John 11:3–6, the disciples and two sisters (Mary and Martha) had to learn to trust God's timing despite their urgent cry for help (v. 3), Christ's perplexing response (v. 4), Christ's affirmation of His personal love, and an unexpected delay (v. 6) that made little sense to any of the parties.

4. For further insight in processing your fears, see *How to Be a Soul Physician*, 239–58.

Part Five

A GRACIOUS, MERCIFUL, AND GOOD GOD WHO IS ALWAYS IN CONTROL

15

God Is Sovereign
HE RULES OVER ALL

*K*ING DAVID had just learned that he would not be building the temple for worshiping the Lord Jehovah. That honor was being given to his son Solomon. Yet David did not complain. Instead, as the time for temple preparation drew near and people brought their offerings to fund the beautiful building, the king exalted in the sovereign, always wise God:

> Yours, O Lord, is the greatness and the power and the glory and the victory and the majesty, indeed everything that is in the heavens and the earth; Yours is the dominion, O Lord, and You exalt Yourself as head over all. Both riches and honor come from You, and You rule over all, and in Your hand is power and might; and it lies in Your hand to make great and to strengthen everyone. Now

therefore, our God, we thank You, and praise Your glorious name.

But who am I and who are my people that we should be able to offer as generously as this? For all things come from You, and from Your hand we have given You. (1 Chronicles 29:11–14)

The Meaning of God's Sovereignty

To say that God is sovereign is to affirm Him as the ruler of His creation who will ultimately accomplish all of His purposes. He is ultimately in control of everything — all resources, all authority, life and death, and every event.

God's Eternal Rule over His Creation, His Redeemed People, and His Coming Kingdom

One way to look at God's rule is to see it in the following three categories: over creation, His redeemed people, and His coming kingdom.

Numerous Scriptures speak of God's creation and describe God as the everlasting King (Psalm 135:13; Jeremiah 10:10; 1 Timothy 1:17) and the ruler of all the kingdoms of the earth (2 Chronicles 20:6). Jesus Christ, God's Son, is called "the King of kings and Lord of lords" (1 Timothy 6:15). The Scriptures also tell us that

- God sits as King forever (Psalms 10:16; 29:10).
- God rules forever (Lamentations 5:19).
- God rules over all (1 Chronicles 29:12).
- God is sovereign over all the nations (Acts 17:24–29).
- God is in control of all authority (Romans 13:1).

This mighty, sovereign God rules over His redeemed people, those who voluntarily submit to Him. In this sense God's people can testify with the psalmist, "You are my King" (Psalm 44:4). When one becomes a Christian, that new believer enters into Christ's kingdom (Colossians 1:13).

One day God the Son will rule after all rebellion is judged. Jesus taught His disciples to pray and anticipate His coming kingdom when His will "will be done, on earth as it is in heaven" (Matthew 6:10). One day He will rule the world with a rod of iron (Revelation 12:5; 19:15; 20:1–6).

The prophets wrote clearly of a messianic king who one day would rule the earth:

And the Lord will be king over all the earth; in that day the Lord will be the only one, and His name the only one. (Zechariah 14:9)

Then the sovereignty, the dominion and the greatness of all the kingdoms under the whole heaven will be given to the people of the saints of the Highest One; His kingdom will be an everlasting kingdom, and all the dominions will serve and obey Him. (Daniel 7:27)

There is a day coming when God will be "all in all" (1 Corinthians 15:28) and every knee will bow to Jesus (Philippians 2:10).

God's Will

In His sovereignty, God always accomplishes His plans. We can look at the accomplishing of His will in three ways.

First, there is His preceptive will. This is what God desires.

In His preceptive will He does not desire evil but rather "desires all men to be saved and to come to the knowledge of the truth" (1 Timothy 2:4).

Second, there is His permissive will. This is what He permits to happen. In His permissive will He allows men to reject Him.

Third, there is His providential will. This is what Ephesians 1:11 speaks of when it declares that He "works all things after the counsel of His will." It is what Romans 8:28 speaks about when it declares that "God causes all things to work together for good . . ."

In His providential will He overrules evil for good. For example, in His preceptive will He does not desire murder. In His permissive will He allowed His Son to be murdered. In His providential will He overruled this awful crime to bring about the greatest blessing the world has ever known.

God desires unity. He allows gossip and slanderous division. He overrules it to reveal those who are truly peacemakers (see 1 Corinthians 11:19).

He created a beautiful paradise. He allowed Satan and man to rebel against Him and bring untold troubles and trials into this world. He overrules these trials in His people's lives to allow them to experience more of His grace and power (2 Corinthians 12:9–10). Richard Wurmbrand wrote the following excerpt in response to all of the unjust suffering in the world.

A legend says that Moses once sat near a well in meditation. A wayfarer stopped to drink from the well, and when he did his purse fell from his girdle into the sand. The man departed. Shortly afterwards another man passed near the well, saw the purse and picked it up.

Later a third man stopped to assuage his thirst and went to sleep in the shadow of the well. Meanwhile, the first man had discovered that his purse was missing and assuming that he must have lost it at the well, returned, awoke the sleeper (who of course knew nothing) and demanded his money back. An argument followed, and irate, the first man killed the latter. Whereupon Moses said to God, "You see, therefore men do not believe in you. There is too much evil and injustice in the world. Why should the first man have lost his purse and then become a murderer? Why should the second have gotten a purse full of gold without having worked for it? The third was completely innocent. Why was he slain?"

God answered, "For once and only once, I will give you an explanation. I cannot do it at every step. The first man was a thief's son. The purse contained money stolen by his father from the father of the second, who, finding the purse, only found what was due him. The third was a murderer whose crime had never been revealed and who received from the first the punishment he deserved. In the future believe that there is sense and righteousness in what transpires even when you do not understand."

Faith in God is the sole answer to the mystery of evil.[1]

As Julian of Norwich notes, "When the end comes and we are taken for judgment above, we will then clearly understand in God the mysteries that puzzle us now. Not one of us will think to say, 'Lord, if it had been some other way, all would be well.'"[2]

God's Sovereignty and Evil

God is described as the King of glory (Psalm 24:8–10), a great King (Psalm 47:2), and a beautiful King (Isaiah 33:17). How could He be truly sovereign if there is so much evil in this world?

God is sovereign over evil in that He is never out of control. If He were, you could not trust Him. However, He is also not blameworthy because of evil. The ultimate answer to the mystery of evil is found in the attributes of God.

- *God is omnipotent* — He rules by His might forever (Psalm 66:7) and is never out of control.
- *God is good* — He is not the blameworthy cause of evil.
- *God is perfect love* — He does not force His way on His creatures but allows them the capacity of choice that is essential to any love relationship.
- *God is sovereign* — He accomplishes His plan in the midst of evil.
- *God is merciful* — He offers His comfort (2 Corinthians 1:3), presence (Matthew 28:20), and example (1 Peter 2:21) to all who look to Him.
- *God is wise* — He can use suffering to enrich one's life (2 Corinthians 4:17–18), brings spiritual maturity (James 1:2–4), disciplines His own (Hebrews 12), and even awakens unbelievers.
- *God is a God of hope* — Christ died to deliver us from evil and suffering, and God will one day judge and confine all evil.

Knowing Him

Five Sovereign Songs

The Bible both affirms and extols the sovereignty of God. Consider these five declarations of the Scriptures, songs of praise and hope.

The pillars of the earth are the Lord's, and He set the world on them. (1 Samuel 2:8)

The Lord has established His throne in the heavens, and His sovereignty rules over all. (Psalm 103:19)

For there is no authority except from God, and those which exist are established by God. (Romans 13:1)

We have obtained an inheritance, having been predestined according to His purpose who works all things after the counsel of His will. (Ephesians 1:11)

He will bring about [Christ's appearing] at the proper time—He who is the blessed and only Sovereign, the King of kings and Lord of lords. (1 Timothy 6:15)

Sovereignty and Man's Responsibility

God is sovereign, and man is still responsible. Within the scope of God's sovereign plan, He has determined to give people the capacity to make responsible choices. Only

a truly sovereign God can give man this capacity and still
never be out of control. Man's responsibility does not com-
promise the truth of God's sovereignty, but rather it magni-
fies the truth of God's sovereignty! Always allow tensions
that you cannot fully understand in your theology in order
to stay biblical.

The apostle Paul strongly affirmed God's sovereignty
(Ephesians 1:3–11; Romans 8:28–9:29). We need to follow his
doctrine and the responsible life that flowed out of it. He
said he was willing to "endure all things for the sake of those
who are chosen, so that they also may obtain the salvation
which is in Christ Jesus and with it eternal glory" (2 Timothy 2:10).

The Bible teaches both the sovereignty of God and the
responsibility of man and sometimes in the same verse. For
example, Peter the apostle explained Christ's death this way:
"This Man, delivered over by the predetermined plan and
foreknowledge of God, you nailed to a cross by the hands of
godless men and put Him to death" (Acts 2:23).

God's Sovereignty Means: Comfort and Confidence

The comforting truth of God's sovereignty is that it is
also consistent with His wisdom, goodness, and righteousness. It is good news to know that evil forces cannot over-
throw God's rule or push Him off His throne even for a
moment. The sovereign God uses evil yet limits it so that
His purposes are ultimately accomplished (cf. Job 1–2; Revelation 9:4–5). Satan and his hosts cannot exert their malice
beyond God's sovereign will. This should give us comfort
and confidence in this world.

Missionaries Jim and Veronica Bowers presented the gospel to Peruvian villagers along the Amazon River, using gospel films and Bible stories, while distributing food and medicine. The couple had served five years when one morning, returning on a missionary flight with their adoptive daughter Charity, they found their plane under attack by the Peruvian Air Force. The military pilot, with faulty information that the Bowers' plane was on an illegal drug run, fired into the small plane. The gunfire killed Veronica and seven-month-old Charity. Jim Bowers and pilot Kevin Donaldson survived in the flaming plane that Donaldson somehow landed on the river.[3]

The deaths seemed senseless. Yet later Bowers would say, "It is the love of God that constrains us to go to the ends of the earth. In the will of God and providence of God, there is no such thing as an 'accident.' He plans everything that comes into our life."[4]

When God's people have been under special pressure, they have turned to their sovereign God to find comfort, just as Jim did. When the Moabites, Ammonites, and Meunites united to defeat Judah, Jehoshaphat sought God and prayed to the ruler of the kings of the earth. He affirmed that "power and might are in Your hand so that no one can stand against You" (2 Chronicles 20:6). He acknowledged, "We are powerless before this great multitude who are coming against us; nor do we know what to do, but our eyes are on You" (v. 12).

In the days of the early church after Peter and John had been arrested and threatened, they went to their companions and lifted their voices to the sovereign creator God.

> And when they heard this, they lifted their voices to God with one accord and said, "O Lord, it is You who

made the heaven and the earth and the sea, and all that is in them, who by the Holy Spirit, through the mouth of our father David Your servant, said, 'Why did the Gentiles rage, and the peoples devise futile things? The kings of the earth took their stand, and the rulers were gathered together against the Lord and against His Christ.'

"For truly in this city there were gathered together against Your holy servant Jesus, whom You anointed, both Herod and Pontius Pilate, along with the Gentiles and the peoples of Israel, to do whatever Your hand and Your purpose predestined to occur." (Acts 4:24–28)

In both cases the sovereign God gloriously heard their prayer and worked on behalf of His people.

There is a comfort and a confidence that comes when you realize that the future is in the hands of our sovereign God who will allow righteousness to eternally triumph (Daniel 2:31–45; 7:1–28; 9:24–27; Revelation 6–22). We need to personalize this confidence so we can say with the psalmist, "My times are in Your hand" (Psalm 31:15).

A believer can face his circumstances with confidence when he acknowledges that events have been ultimately arranged for God's sovereign purposes. Life is not to be viewed as a series of accidents but rather as a series of divine appointments. What man may mean for evil, God can overrule for good (Genesis 50:20; Romans 8:28). As has often been declared, our disappointments can be viewed as His appointments. His people are His treasure, and He guards them as the apple of His eye (Psalm 17:8).

One day a blizzard hit London and a fifteen-year-old boy named Charles was not able to make it to his own church. He entered a small Primitive Methodist Church with no speaker and only a few people present. With the preacher absent, one man took it upon himself to speak to the few and read Isaiah 45:22 — "Look unto me, and be ye saved, all the ends of the earth" (KJV).

Grasping for something to say, the gentleman kept repeating the text and pointing his bony finger at young Charles. "Look, young man! Look! Look to Christ!" On the way home he did look, and this young man became one of the greatest preachers in church history — Charles Spurgeon.[5] The weather was unfavorable, the young man could not make it to his regular church, the preacher did not even make it, and the speaker was somewhat inept; but the sovereign God won a great victory.

We can be confident because He is ruling. The Ruler of the kings of the earth loves us (see Revelation 1:5)!

God's Sovereignty Means: Being Accountable to God

All authority is accountable to God. Whether a king, a president, or a prime minister, any authority needs to realize that he or she has been placed there by the sovereign permission of God. He is the "head over all rule and authority" (Colossians 2:10), and He can dethrone one or strip one of their authority at any moment (Luke 1:52). King Nebuchadnezzar, the most powerful man on the earth at that time, learned this in quite a profound way (Daniel 4:17, 25; 5:21).

Everyone must give an account of how they use the authority God has given to them. For example, all employers will have to give an account as to whether or not they paid fair wages to their employees (Malachi 3:5).

One is also accountable to God for how he uses the gifts he

has received. There is nothing that we have that has not been given to us by our sovereign God (1 Corinthians 4:7). All of our gifts, abilities, talents, resources, and opportunities are gifts that we are to use to serve our sovereign God and His purposes.

A failure to realize our accountability to God results in a variety of sinful attitudes. Here are some of these:

- *Pride*—Taking credit for what God has graciously given us.
- A *critical and judgmental attitude*—Setting ourselves up as the final judge of another.
- A *grumbling and lack of contentment; being jealous*—Failing to realize God's wisdom and eternal loving purposes behind our lot in life.
- A *lack of reverence*—Failure to worship and obey the King of kings and Lord of lords.

God's Sovereignty Means:
Hope in Trials

As long as we submit to God's authority, we can expect some constructive purpose to come out of any trial (Romans 8:28). We will not understand all of God's providential dealings this side of heaven, though we can humbly petition Him to share with us the insight that we need to know to see His good hand in the circumstance.

God's Sovereignty Means:
Prayers for Our Leaders

The Scripture tells us, "The king's heart is like channels of water in the hand of the Lord; He turns it wherever He wishes" (Proverbs 21:1). Since "the king's heart is . . . in the hand of the Lord," the most important priority of the gathered church is to pray.

That was the plea of Paul: "First of all, then, I urge that entreaties and prayers, petitions and thanksgivings, be made on behalf of all men, for kings and all who are in authority, so that we may lead a tranquil and quiet life in all godliness and dignity" (1 Timothy 2:1–2).

It is not our responsibility to govern the world. It is our responsibility to be available to our sovereign God and pray for those He has placed in authority. As we pray we are to sing praises to the Lord (Psalm 47:6) and rejoice in our King (Psalm 149:2). He alone is the King of kings and Lord of lords!

Notes

1. Richard Wurmbrand, "Why All the Suffering?" *The Voice of the Martyrs*, October 1999, 10.

2. Julian of Norwich, *Christianity Today*, September 2006, 112.

3. Amanda Ripley, "A Mission Interrupted," *Time*, April 29, 2001, at www.time.com/time/magazine/article/0,9171,107933,00.html; and "CIA Takes Fault in 2001 Missionary Plane Shooting," Mission Network News, 3 November 2010, at www.mnnonline.org/article/14923.

4. Quoted in *Pulse*, 1 June 2001, 2. The story of Jim and Veronica (Roni) Bowers is told in Kristen Stagg, *If God Should Choose* (Chicago: Moody, 2002).

5. Robert J. Morgan, *On This Day: 365 Amazing and Inspiring Stories about Saints, Martyrs & Heroes* (Nashville: Nelson, 1997), January 6.

16

God Is Merciful

HE WANTS YOU TO EXPERIENCE HIS MERCY

*O*NE OF GOD'S very names is "the Father of mercies and God of all comfort" (2 Corinthians 1:3). His "mercies are over all His works" (Psalm 145:9), and God will shine upon us His "tender mercy" (Luke 1:78).

Men and women alike have weaknesses and experience miseries, and God has a pity for our helpless condition. His mercy is His deep, inward feeling that identifies with the helpless and afflicted, and that expresses itself in compassionate help to relieve their state. A mother's love for her nursing baby and a father's love for his children are a small reflection of God's mercy.

What's the Difference
between Mercy and Grace?

It has often been said that God's grace is His giving us what we do not deserve, and His mercy as God withholding from us what we do deserve. While there is truth in the above statement, it fails to do full justice to God's mercy. For example, when the Good Samaritan offered help to the one in need, he is said to have shown mercy (Luke 10:37). If you tried to plug the above definition into this verse, it would not fit.

The distinction between grace and mercy is the different focus of each one. God's grace is the favor that He shows to each of us in our guilt. God's mercy is the compassion that He gives to us in our misery. Both are attributes of the same wonderful God but carry a slightly different focus. We will look at God's grace in depth in chapter 17; at present, let's consider His mercy and how it can be active in our lives.

Descriptions of His Mercy

God visits His needy people with His tender mercy (Luke 1:78). While we were dead, enslaved, and condemned (Ephesians 2:1–3), the God who is "rich in mercy" gave us spiritual life (Ephesians 2:4–5) and spiritual authority (Ephesians 2:6). No one deserves God's mercy, which is described as both sovereignly given—"I will have mercy on whom I have mercy" (Romans 9:15)—and entirely unmerited—"for God has shut up all in disobedience so that He may show mercy to all" (Romans 11:32).

How to Experience God's Mercy

While mercy is in no way merited by us, we are to humble ourselves and look to God for His mercy. Here are the directions that the Scripture gives in order for one to do that.

Those who admit their need for God's mercy understand that they are by their very nature "children of wrath" (Ephesians 2:3). Only God who is rich in mercy can save us (Ephesians 2:4–5). So we plead with God "in wrath [to] remember mercy" (Habakkuk 3:2). *We receive God's mercy by first admitting we need it.* As we walk with God as His child, we admit our need of God's merciful aid. We realize that we are in a battle and must depend upon our merciful God. King David credited God for his victories (for example, see Psalm 18:17).

Even in the area of guidance, we must rely upon our merciful Shepherd to lead us for His name's sake. As Jeremiah wrote, " I know, O Lord, that a man's way is not in himself, nor is it in a man who walks to direct his steps" (Jeremiah 10:23). Admitting our need is the most basic step in experiencing the mercy of God.

A second way we experience God's mercy is by fearing (honoring) God. The Scriptures tell us that God's mercy is granted those who fear God: "Just as a father has compassion on his children, so the Lord has compassion on those who fear Him" (Psalm 103:13). "His mercy is upon generation after generation toward those who fear Him" (Luke 1:50).

More about the Fear of the Lord

The fear of God is a grand and glorious subject. Let me suggest that at some point in your life you study this important topic. You may choose, as I have done, to organize your insights under these three categories.

First, what it means to fear God. Take advantage of the psalmist's invitation, "Come, you children, listen to me; I will teach you the fear of the Lord" (Psalm 34:11). Remember that Israel was told to fear God and in the same verse was told to not be afraid (Exodus 20:20). Fear in God is always associated with obeying God and hating evil. One thing that has helped me is to remember that God has told me to fear Him and to trust Him. I am afraid of some people, but I do not trust them either. An appropriate fear of God will also be consistent with trusting, loving, and delighting in Him.

Second, the benefits of fearing God. The man who fears God is said to be blessed (Psalm 112:1)! All of Psalm 112 is a list of the benefits of the fear of God. Just as delighting in the Lord is a pathway to experience the desires of your heart, so the same thing can be said about fearing the Lord. Those who fear the Lord will not lack anything they need to do God's will (Psalm 34:9).

Third, how to develop the fear of God. "The fear of the Lord" is viewed as a parallel phrase with the "knowledge of God" (Proverbs 2:5). As we get to know God in His full-orbed revelation of Himself, we will develop a fear of the Lord. Remember, *all* aspects of God's character play a part in developing a fear of the Lord. For example, if we realize we live in the presence of an all-knowing God, we learn to live our life before Him. The psalmist also expressed how the forgiveness of God produced a fear of the Lord (see Psalm 130:3–4)! A balanced understanding of God's character produces a fear of the Lord.

The promise God makes to Israel in Jeremiah should encourage us.

I will give them one heart and one way, that they may fear
Me always, for their own good and for the good of their
children after them. I will make an everlasting covenant
with them that I will not turn away from them, to do
them good; and I will put the fear of Me in their hearts
so that they will not turn away from Me. (32:39–40)

This passage about the future restoration of Israel offers
a truth about the way of God: He can put the fear of Himself
in a heart. Our response in faith is to ask Him to do it for us.
As the Scripture says of the ungodly, "there is no fear of God
before their eyes" (Psalm 36:1; Romans 3:18). God's greater
concern is when there is no fear of Him in His church. Trust
Him to put the fear of Himself in your life, for this is the
pathway to experiencing His mercy.

Learn to Look to God for His Mercy

The mercy of God is available for us in many areas. First
and foremost, His mercy *begins with our spiritual salvation.*
His sovereign mercy moves God to give spiritual life to those
who are dead so that they can be born again (Ephesians 2:4;
Titus 3:5; 1 Peter 1:3). Once we die and experience God's
judgment, it is too late to cry for mercy (see Luke 16:24–26).

God's mercy *continues in His merciful plans for us.* Paul
attributed not only his salvation to the mercy of God but also
God putting him into service (1 Timothy 1:12–13). Even in
2 Corinthians 4:1, he talks about the ministry that he has
because of God's mercy. Apart from God's mercy all of us
would waste our lives. It is easy to be tempted to pursue
something that in no way is fitted for our life. God's good
works that He has prepared beforehand for us (Ephesians

2:10) are an extension of His merciful call on our life. This is not to say that His plan is easy, but it is to say that it fits us because it is designed for us.

I think of a missionary whom my family and I have visited on multiple occasions in Mexico. As I minister in the church he has planted, the camp he has built, and the business he has started, I see a man living out God's merciful plan. I simply could not envision him in a typical pastorate in his home country. It would be like making a guide dog pull a child's wagon. It is not that the dog would not be fully capable, but it would not be the best fit for his specific gifts. Look to God for His merciful and wise plan for you!

Mercy Available for Transforming Our Character

The apostle Paul did not hesitate to declare that in himself he was not adequate for the task God had given him. In fact he said that it was only because of the mercy that he received that he did not lose heart (2 Corinthians 4:1). This mercy he received seems to be referring to the merciful renewing of his inner man day by day (2 Corinthians 4:16). The believer does not have to be adequate in himself to keep going. We just need to be humble enough to admit our need and come boldly to God's throne of grace and find the merciful and gracious help we need moment by moment (Hebrews 4:16). This was the encouragement that Paul gave to Timothy when he prayed for him to experience God's "grace, mercy and peace" in the midst of overseeing the churches in Ephesus (1 Timothy 1:2; 2 Timothy 1:2).

This merciful renewing work of the Spirit can also transform our character. Paul gave credit to God's mercy for transforming him into a trustworthy man (1 Corinthians 7:25).

Mercy for Healing and for Comfort

His mercy also can bring healing and support. When Paul's friend Epaphroditus was sick to the point of death, God's merciful intervention in his life restored him to health. Paul regarded his friend's healing both as God's mercy to Epaphroditus and to Paul himself, to keep him from intense sorrow (Philippians 2:27).

When one is sick we are to trust them to the merciful care of God. In this case, God mercifully healed Epaphroditus. This is not the will of God in every case. If it were, no one would ever die, but it is always His will to be a God of mercy to us in our need.

God's merciful support extends not only to the sick person but also to the people concerned about the sick person. In the case of Epaphroditus, God knew that his life was a merciful provision for Paul at this time. To do God's will all we need is our Lord and what He in His mercy chooses to provide. We look to His mercy in our times of physical need and our loved one's need. We also rest in the truth that if God takes one of our loved ones home, He will be there to mercifully fill the hole that has been left. Praise God that He is a God of mercy!

God's mercy includes offering us His comfort. In fact, Paul calls Him "the Father of mercies and God of all comfort" (2 Corinthians 1:3). God's merciful comfort will always be sufficient (2 Corinthians 1:5)! In fact it will not only be sufficient for us but also for us to overflow to others with the comfort that we have received (2 Corinthians 1:4, 6).

Do we ever have to fear what might happen? No, because God has promised that His merciful comfort will be there for us, and it will always be sufficient.

Mercy to Help in Your Spiritual Battles

The psalmist credits God for delivering him from his strong enemy and those who hated him. God in His mercy did this because "they were too mighty for me" (Psalm 18:17). The New Testament gives clear revelation of the spiritual battle in which the believer is engaged (Ephesians 6:10–12). For this reason we see people in their need coming to Jesus for His merciful help. Here are two accounts from the Gospel according to Matthew:

> A Canaanite woman from that region came out and began to cry out, saying, "Have mercy on me, Lord, Son of David; my daughter is cruelly demon-possessed." (Matthew 15:22)

> Lord, have mercy on my son, for he is a lunatic and is very ill; for he often falls into the fire and often into the water. (Matthew 17:15)

God in His mercy can give us insight into understanding Satan's schemes (2 Corinthians 2:11; see Table 5, p. 133) and in appropriating God's strength and armor in our battle today (Ephesians 6:10–18). Appeal to His mercy to uncover any lie that the Evil One is tempting you to believe and to lead you to His merciful truth that can replace this lie and set you free.

Becoming a
Person of Mercy

Once we realize that our need (Ephesians 2:1–3) was such that only a merciful God (Ephesians 2:4) could save us, we can surely understand that it is appropriate to "glorify God for His mercy" (Romans 15:9).

One way to offer Him such glory is to demonstrate mercy ourselves. In fact, that is the command of our Lord Jesus to His disciples then and now:

> Be merciful, just as your Father is merciful. Do not judge, and you will not be judged; and do not condemn, and you will not be condemned; pardon, and you will be pardoned. Give, and it will be given to you. They will pour into your lap a good measure—pressed down, shaken together, and running over. For by your standard of measure it will be measured to you in return. (Luke 6:36–38)

These words of Jesus teach us several important elements in showing mercy to others. A merciful person

- *is not judgmental and condemning.* Instead, a person of mercy gives people what they need and not what they deserve (cf. Luke 18:9–14).
- *is not unforgiving and bitter.* Instead, a person of mercy extends to others what has been mercifully extended to him (Matthew 18:21–35).
- *is not stingy.* Instead, a person of mercy is generous to others (Luke 6:38).

Ask God for His wisdom, which is characterized by mercy (James 3:17). The one who sows mercy will reap it (cf. Matthew 5:7; James 2:13). "Truly a merciful man does himself good" (Proverbs 11:17).

Present Your Life to a God of Mercy

The mercies of God refer to His merciful character and the infinite riches that He has provided for His people in Christ. The Scripture calls each of us to present our life to this God of mercy, to become "a living and holy sacrifice, acceptable to God" (Romans 12:1).

It is a very logical response to present your life to this God of mercy. Who else would you want to present your life to? He has mercifully accepted us in Christ (Romans 5:1–2) and even mercifully made it possible to present our lives to Him (Romans 6:11–13). He takes care of what has been presented to Him for He is "able to guard" what is entrusted to Him (2 Timothy 1:12). Nothing is more secure than placing every part of your being and every part of your life in the merciful hands of God.[1]

Note

1. For more insight into experiencing the truth of Romans 12:1, see Bill Thrasher, *How to Be a Soul Physician* (Seattle: CreateSpace, 2010), 287–93. The book can be found at the author's website, www.victoriouspraying. com.

17

God Is Gracious

WE OWE EVERYTHING
TO HIS GRACE

*A*FTER TALKING WITH his father, Jonathan Edwards took a contemplative walk through a pasture. He wrote,

> I walked abroad alone, in a solitary place in my father's pasture, for contemplation. And as I was walking there, and looked up on the sky and clouds; there came into my mind, a sweet sense of the glorious majesty and grace of God, that I know not how to express. I seemed to see them both in a sweet conjunction: majesty and meekness joined together: it was a sweet, and gentle, and holy majesty; and also a majestic meekness; an awful sweetness; a high, and great, and holy gentleness.[1]

We see in Edwards's contemplation something of the beautiful balance of God's character. We should never play one attribute against another, for both are describing the essence and character of the one true God. Still, we cannot deny that God manifests grace in all His actions. God is the "God of all grace" (1 Peter 5:10). The very essence of God is gracious, and for this reason we read about the grace of God (Luke 2:40), the grace of our Lord Jesus Christ (Revelation 22:21), and the Spirit of grace (Zechariah 12:10). He is gracious and also gives grace (Psalm 84:11).

So what is God's grace? Grace is the favor that He shows through the merit of Christ to those who deserve only His wrath. Because He is gracious, Martin Luther said that God's love "turns in the direction where it does not find good which it may enjoy, but where it may confer good upon the bad and needy person."

Description of God's Grace

God's grace is described as *abounding* (Romans 5:15), *abundant* (Romans 5:17), and even *more than abundant* (1 Timothy 1:14) as it triumphs over sin. It is also described as *sufficient* in that it is powerful enough for us to deal with any circumstances that have been entrusted to us (2 Corinthians 12:9). God is both sovereign and generous in freely bestowing His grace upon us (Ephesians 1:4–6).

God's grace is so valuable that the Scriptures speak of "the surpassing riches of His grace" (Ephesians 2:7). The experience of His grace is something that will be enjoyed for all eternity, "in the ages to come" for all to see that He is a gracious God (Ephesians 2:7).

The attribute of grace and the gifts that flow from His

grace have been abused by some. Some have seen it as that which gives one a license to sin and live in any way they please (Romans 6:1; Jude 4). This is not the "true grace of God" (1 Peter 5:12), which transforms our lives into new people and teaches us to live godly (Titus 2:11–12). Those who have truly experienced it will praise His glorious grace (Ephesians 1:6).

God's Grace Should
Lead to a Grateful Heart

What have we earned from God? We have earned God's righteous judgment! Our sin—and all of us have sinned (Romans 3:23)—has earned God's wrath. When you realize that all you ever have received or will receive other than judgment is due to the grace of God, only then can you begin to truly develop a grateful heart. Martyn Lloyd Jones said that "the ultimate test of our spirituality is our amazement at the grace of God."

It is the grace of God that motivated Christ to taste death for us (Hebrews 2:9). This is why the good news of His death and resurrection is called the "gospel of the grace of God" (Acts 20:24). Grace is merited to us only through Christ (John 1:17; Romans 1:5), and we owe everything to this grace that has called us into relationship with God (Galatians 1:6).

Most of us have what I call lines of expectations. We unconsciously or consciously think that we deserve some things: good health, respect from others, a comfortable life, etc. When we get over and above these expectations, we are grateful. The problem is that these expectations set us up to be bitter. In God's plan some of His servants do not enjoy good health or live a long life—and all will suffer trials. When we realize that all of God's blessings — even those we do not understand — are extensions of His grace, we begin to learn the secret of continual thanks.

When Bible commentator Matthew Henry was robbed, he wrote in his journal four reasons why he could thank God:

(1) I've never been robbed before.
(2) He took my purse and not my life.
(3) He took all that I had, but I did not have very much.
(4) I was robbed, but it was not I who robbed.[2]

The presence of genuine gratitude in a life is evidence of the Holy Spirit's control (Ephesians 5:18–20). It is the Spirit who teaches us of our true need and indebtedness to God's grace. He opens our eyes to see God as the author of every good and perfect gift — every kindness extended to us, every mouthful of food, every moment of rest, and every beneficial experience. The act of thanksgiving is a response to the Holy Spirit's work in our life!

Grace Shown in Our Salvation

To say that salvation is unearned is true in that it is not earned by us. However, it came at great expense to our Savior. He *earned* our salvation and freely gave it to us. It is based on His work and not on our work. This truth recurs in Paul's biblical writings.

Being justified as a gift by His grace through the redemption which is in Christ Jesus. (Romans 3:24)

But to the one who does not work, but believes in Him who justifies the ungodly, his faith is credited as righteousness. (Romans 4:5)

But if it is by grace, it is no longer on the basis of works, otherwise grace is no longer grace. (Romans 11:6)

For by grace you have been saved through faith; and that not of yourselves, it is the gift of God; not as a result of works, so that no one may boast. (Ephesians 2:8–9)

Who has saved us and called us with a holy calling, not according to our works, but according to His own purpose and grace which was granted us in Christ Jesus from all eternity. (2 Timothy 1:9)

Perhaps you have heard about the man who dies and goes to heaven. Of course, St. Peter meets him at the pearly gates. St. Peter says, "Here's how it works. You need one hundred points to make it into heaven. You tell me all the good things you've done, and I give you a certain number of points for each item, depending on how good it was. When you reach one hundred points, you get in."

"Okay," the man says, "I was married to the same woman for fifty years and never cheated on her, even in my heart."

"That's wonderful," says St. Peter. "That's worth three points!"

"Three points?" he says. "Well, I attended church all my life and supported its ministry with my tithe and service."

"Terrific!" says St. Peter. "That's certainly worth a point."

"One point? I started a soup kitchen in my city and worked in a shelter for homeless veterans."

"Fantastic, that's good for two more points," he says.
"Two points!" the man cries. "At this rate the only way
I get into heaven is by the grace of God."
"Bingo, one hundred points! Come on in!"

Grace as the
Basis for the Christian Life

A Christian is one who stands in God's grace. Martyn
Lloyd Jones's sermon on Romans 5:1–11 helped me to understand the idea of standing in God's grace. Viewing a beautiful glorious palace, the miserable man who lived on the
streets saw the festive activities and bountiful provisions
that those in the palace enjoyed day after day. Meanwhile, he
shivered in the cold, longing for food. One day the son of the
king came to him, took him by the hand, and introduced
him to his father, the king. Providing royal garments for him,
he told him that he could enjoy permanent favor and access
to the king, as if he were the king's son.

Do you see the gospel analogy? If you are a genuine
believer in Christ, God loves you with the same intensity as
His own Son (John 17:23 — look it up!). Do you see yourself
as one who is loved by the King of kings and who has continual and permanent access to Him and His spiritual riches
because of His Son? Or do you see yourself as the pathetic
man on the street? You may live physically on the street, but
if you know Jesus, you can enjoy the King's palace. You may
have millions of dollars in this world, but if you do not
acknowledge Jesus, you are living in great poverty.

Many people are outside the church today because we
who are Christians represent the Christian life so poorly.
Many Christians are living as spiritual paupers when we

were meant to live as children of the heavenly King. God says that because of the Lord Jesus' perfect life and cruel death, a follower of Jesus can enjoy peace with God and a permanent standing in His favor! Do you agree with this truth and rest in His favor? God is not pleased if you do not agree with this truth. Such a decision would not be a sign of humility but rather of rebellion. The Christian is to be a humble person, but humility is submitting to God and agreeing with Him.

A believer is now said to be "under the reign of grace" (see Romans 5:17, 21) and under grace (Romans 6:14). What does this mean? There are four implications to living under God's grace.

First, living under grace means to be accepted by God's grace. Every other religion in the world tells one to obey in order to be accepted. God says our obedience is a response to the truth that we have already been accepted. Listen to how William Newell articulated the truth of being under grace:

1. The believer is not "on probation." He has been accepted in Christ.
2. To believe and to commit to be loved while unworthy is the great secret.
3. The believer can expect to be blessed, though he realizes more and more his lack of worth.
4. The believer can testify of God's goodness at all times.
5. The believer can rely on God's chastening hand as a mark of His kindness.[3]

Second, living under God's grace involves the gracious gift of having the authority to live a new life. The reaction to the message of grace is that if you tell others that they can rest in

God's love and acceptance, they may cognitively understand the message of God's grace but not be changed by this grace. In contrast, those who have truly embraced God's grace will be changed into new people who can now live a transformed life (Romans 6:1–14).

Knowing Him

And Grace Was Free

William Newell, assistant superintendent at Moody Bible Institute under President R. A. Torrey and a renowned Bible commentator, explored the doctrine of grace in his classic study *Romans*. In addition to the five truths of being under grace noted on page 237, Newell explained how belief in God's grace can rid us of disappointment, discouragement, and pride, and can lead us to true devotion:

1. To be disappointed with yourself is to have believed in yourself.
2. To be discouraged is unbelief regarding God's purpose and plan of blessing for you.
3. To be proud is to be blind! For we have no standing before God in ourselves.
4. The lack of divine blessing comes from unbelief and not from failure of devotion.
5. Real devotion to God arises, not from man's will to show it, but from the discovery that blessing has been received from God while we were yet unworthy and undevoted to Him.

Newell also wrote the classic hymn "At Calvary," with its great refrain that begins, "Mercy there was great, and grace was free."

He knew the cross is where God most demonstrated His magnificent grace.

Third, living under God's grace involves the gift of God's gracious enablement. This is why most of Paul's epistles begin with the greeting and prayer that the readers would continue to experience God's grace. Good deeds done in the flesh will lose their ability to stimulate you and will leave you feeling very empty. However, when we do these deeds with the aid of God's gracious provision of the Spirit, we can be both stimulated and richly satisfied.

Fourth, living under grace also involves using the gracious provision of the blood of Christ to continually cleanse us as we walk in the light (1 John 1:7–9). God does not desire us to sin, but He has graciously provided a way that we can be restored and walk in fellowship with Him as we confess our transgressions to Him.[4]

Grace for Growing in the Christian Life

The message of the apostles was for Christians to continue in the grace of God (Acts 13:43). To "fall from grace" is to revert back to a works and law mentality (Galatians 5:4). Paul, for example, called believers who tried to live for Christ only through personal effort "foolish," writing, "Are you so foolish? Having begun by the Spirit, are you now being perfected by the flesh?" (Galatians 3:3).

Paul credited the grace of God for motivating and empowering all of his labor: "By the grace of God I am what I am, and His grace toward me did not prove vain; but I

labored even more than all of them, yet not I, but the grace
of God with me" (1 Corinthians 15:10).

For this reason Paul urged Timothy to be strong in grace
(2 Timothy 2:1). This is not a theoretical theological concept.
It is rather the gracious motivating and enabling work of
God that makes it possible for one to do his work not only
because one has to but because one wants to (1 Peter 5:2)!
Lasting motivation must come from within (Philemon 14).

Grace for Every Aspect of Our Lives

The grace of God is available for every aspect of our lives.
Look at how the Scriptures speak of this grace. It is available for prayer, for greater faith, for our marriage, for ministry, for giving, for suffering, and in receiving spiritual gifts.
His grace is available for our prayers.

I will pour out on the house of David and on the inhabi-
tants of Jerusalem, the Spirit of grace and of supplication,
so that they will look on Me whom they have pierced; and
they will mourn for Him, as one mourns for an only son,
and they will weep bitterly over Him like the bitter weep-
ing over a firstborn. (Zechariah 12:10)

Therefore let us draw near with confidence to the throne
of grace, so that we may receive mercy and find grace to
help in time of need. (Hebrews 4:16; note how the
psalmist appeals to God's grace as well. See Psalms 4:1;
9:13; 25:16.)

His grace is available for greater faith. "And when he wanted
to go across to Achaia, the brethren encouraged him and

wrote to the disciples to welcome him; and when he had
arrived, he greatly helped those who had believed through
grace" (Acts 18:27).

His grace is available for our marriage. "You husbands in the
same way, live with your wives in an understanding way, as
with someone weaker, since she is a woman; and show her
honor as a fellow heir of the grace of life, so that your prayers
will not be hindered" (1 Peter 3:7).

His grace is available for ministry. "Recognizing the grace
that had been given to me, James and Cephas and John, who
were reputed to be pillars, gave to me and Barnabas the right
hand of fellowship, so that we might go to the Gentiles and
they to the circumcised" (Galatians 2:9; see also Ephesians 3:2,
7, 8).

His grace is available for giving.

Now, brethren, we wish to make known to you the grace
of God which has been given in the churches of Mace-
donia. (2 Corinthians 8:1)

But just as you abound in everything, in faith and utter-
ance and knowledge and in all earnestness and in the
love we inspired in you, see that you abound in this gracious work also. (2 Corinthians 8:7)

His grace is available for our suffering. "For to you it has been
granted for Christ's sake, not only to believe in Him, but also
to suffer for His sake" (Philippians 1:29).

His grace provides our spiritual gifts. "We have gifts that
differ according to the grace given to us" (Romans 12:6).
Paul tells those at the church at Ephesus, "To each one of us
grace was given according to the measure of Christ's gift"

(Ephesians 4:7). Peter calls these gifts expressions of God's "manifold grace": "As each one has received a special gift, employ it in serving one another as good stewards of the manifold grace of God" (1 Peter 4:10).

We grow in this experience of God's grace as we humble ourselves before God and admit our need for His provision, motivation, and enablement in all areas of our lives (1 Peter 5:5; James 4:6). At times God even sends providential circumstances into our lives that aid us in humbling ourselves in order to experience more of this grace (2 Chronicles 12:9–12).

Humble yourself at this very moment and come to His throne of grace for whatever your need may be today. Remember the words of Hebrews 4:16: "Therefore let us draw near with confidence to the throne of grace, so that we may receive mercy and find grace to help in time of need."

The Best Is Yet to Come

As we get to know the God of grace, keep in mind the best is always yet to come. In fact, the God of all grace has graciously promised and provided for us a glorious future experience of His grace. That grace culminates in the return of Christ to earth for His people. It is here that we are to fix our hope:

> Therefore, prepare your minds for action, keep sober in spirit, fix your hope completely on the grace to be brought to you at the revelation of Jesus Christ. (1 Peter 1:13)

Notes

1. Jonathan Edwards, *Resolutions of a Saintly Scholar* (Minneapolis: World Wide Publications, 1992), 12.

2. Reprinted in *Coronet*, vol. 17 (1944); as cited at wikiquote: http://en. wikiquote.org/wiki/Matthew_Henry.

3. William R. Newell, *Romans* (Chicago: Moody, 1938, 1976), 246–47. Newell included five additional truths about being under grace, as shown in the sidebar "And Grace Was Free" in this chapter.

4. For more information on these four truths, see Bill Thrasher, *How to Be a Soul Physician* (Seattle: CreateSpace, 2010); available at www.victorious praying.com.

18

God Is Good

NO ONE IS GOOD
BUT GOD ALONE

*J*ESUS' RESPONSE to the rich young ruler came in the form of a question: "Why do you call Me good? No one is good except God alone" (Mark 10:18).

If goodness is unique to God, in what ways does God display goodness? Here are four ways God alone is good:

1. Only God is infinitely good — His goodness will never be exhausted.
2. Only God is perfectly good — He could never be better.
3. Only God is immutably good — His goodness will not change.
4. Only God is the source of all goodness — Barnabas is described as a good man (Acts 11:24), but his goodness is a gift of God because in our depraved state there is "none who does good" (Romans 3:12).

What *Goodness* Means

Goodness speaks generally of the moral perfection of God. "Good and upright is the Lord" (Psalm 25:8), and His very name is good (Psalm 52:9). In particular, His goodness speaks of His unchanging disposition of kindness, generosity, and holy pleasure in the joy of His people. He rejoices over His people to do them good (Deuteronomy 30:9; Jeremiah 32:41).

God is the most winsome, or *pleasing*, of all beings. He is better than the best of men. He is even better than your most ideal thought of any other delightful thing or person. His goodness is described as abundant (Psalm 145:7) and great (Nehemiah 9:25).

Men and women look to idols in order to meet the thirst of their hearts. But if one is convinced that God is altogether good, he or she will recognize the folly of drinking out of the polluted wells of sin instead of coming to Jesus to quench their thirst (John 7:37–39). For example, after King David drank from the wrong stream and suffered God's rebuke, he recognized his folly and repented (2 Samuel 12:7–9, 13).[1]

The only appropriate response is to praise the Lord who is good and whose name is lovely (Psalm 135:3). Let all His good gifts of provisions, friendships, and help from others give you a small taste of His goodness.

The Goodness of Our Giving God

Our good God is a giving God who desires us to know His fellowship, which is restful to our souls. As C. S. Lewis says, "In God there is no hunger that needs to be filled, only plenteousness that desires to give." God gives to us in the following ways.

Our God Gives
Generously and without Reproach

God is said to give generously and without reproach or finding fault (James 1:5). There may have been times when you had a need and also knew individuals who could meet that need if you asked them. However, your reluctance to ask is because along with the gift you will also receive an "I told you so." They would give but not without finding fault. God gives generously and without reproach.

Our Good God Gives
Good and Perfect Gifts

God gives good gifts (James 1:17). These good gifts come from His good storehouse, which He opens. He describes the gift of a wife (Proverbs 18:22) and the gift of children (Genesis 30:20) as good. The promises that He gives are good (Joshua 21:45) because they can be trusted. His hope is a good hope (2 Thessalonians 2:16) because it will not lead you to be disappointed. His Word (Jeremiah 29:10; Hebrews 6:5), His way (1 Samuel 12:23), and His will (Romans 12:2) are all good because they spring from His good pleasure (Philippians 2:13).

A good gift is one that is useful and beneficial from God's perspective. Jesus said, "If you then, being evil, know how to give good gifts to your children, how much more will your Father who is in heaven give what is good to those who ask Him" (Matthew 7:11).

God's gifts are described as "good" and "perfect" (James 1:17). They are perfect in that they are complete and not a partial gift. It is for this reason that the gifts that flow from His goodness truly satisfy (Psalm 65:4).

Our Good God
Continues to Give All Gifts

Every good and perfect gift comes from God (see James 1:17). Every mouthful of food, moment of peace, act of kindness toward us—every gift small and great is ultimately from our God. Never become infatuated with the gifts but rather with the Giver.

God has already given the greatest gift—His Son. With God we can rest in the truth that He will continue to give all we will ever need (Romans 8:32; see also 1 Corinthians 3:21–23). When you are tempted to lust for something or someone, answer this temptation with the faith that says God has a righteous way to meet this need. When you are tempted to covet what another has, respond by affirming that God will give you everything you need to do His will.

After praying over 1 Corinthians 3:21–23 for a year, I came to the conclusion that we can trust God to provide everything we will ever need—and not be one second late—to complete God's plan on this earth. In this way the victory that overcomes the world is faith in a good God (1 John 5:5).

God's Ways Are Good

Learning God's ways is the pathway to getting to know God (Exodus 33:13). One who learns God's ways gets to experience the goodness of God. In contrast, one who rejects God's ways brings himself harm.

Keep the Lord's commandments and His statutes which I am commanding you today for your good. (Deuteronomy 10:13)

He who sins against me injures himself; all those who hate me love death. (Proverbs 8:36)

The Scriptures tell us that when we fear God and accept His ways as good, it brings good to both us and our descendants.

And I will give them one heart and one way, that they may fear Me always, for their own good and for the good of their children after them. (Jeremiah 32:39)

How great is Your goodness, which You have stored up for those who fear You, which You have wrought for those who take refuge in You, before the sons of men! (Psalm 31:19)

Seeking God Leads to Lacking No Good Thing

King David, who grew up as a shepherd boy, knew how God provides all things, declaring, "The young lions do lack and suffer hunger; but they who seek the Lord shall not be in want of any good thing" (Psalm 34:10).

The promise of a good God is that if you do the primary thing, you will get the secondary thing. The primary thing is to follow the Lord God in faith.

Note the positive outcome of walking uprightly in Psalm 84:11.

Note the positive outcome of delighting in the Lord in Psalm 37:4.

Note the positive outcome of seeking first Christ's kingdom and His righteousness in Matthew 6:33.

If you seek the secondary things, you are not promised that you will get them, and you will miss the primary thing.

God's Gifts May
Come in Strange Packages

In experiencing God's good gifts, you may need to expand your understanding of good. Those things described as "good" in Romans 8:28 are defined in verse 29 as that which conforms us to the image of Christ. For this reason there are times we need to experience the good gift of God's loving discipline (Deuteronomy 8:15–16; Psalm 119:71; Hebrews 12:10).

It is not often that you hear someone asking for the good gift of loneliness; however, if it causes you to seek the companionship of God, it is good. Anything that encourages you to seek God is a good gift (2 Chronicles 26:5).

The goodness of our spiritual battles is that they teach us our dependence on Christ. The goodness of our trials is that they allow us to experience the God of all comfort. As God seeks to eternally enrich your life, you may need that perspective to see the goodness in some of His gifts. In the end we will see that God's will is good, and it is exactly what we would always want if we knew all the facts.

How God Displays His Goodness

Although we may not always understand how God's goodness works to our good in a specific situation, in many ways God displays His goodness in our daily lives. We can see His goodness in all His works, for all that He does is good. In particular, God's goodness is displayed in His creation, His providential care, the advent of Christ, and bringing us to repentance.

The Scriptures tell us that everything God created is good (Genesis 1:31; 1 Timothy 4:4). God is good to all (Psalm 145:9) and satisfies His creation with good (Psalm 104:24–28). Even an unbeliever experiences the goodness of God's provisions (see Acts 14:17). God's kind restraint of sin allows there to be some order in a world that is not submissive to the Creator.

God displays His goodness in Christ and in bringing us to repentance. The kindness or goodness of God appeared in Christ (Titus 3:4), and hundreds of years earlier Isaiah had prophesied of the good gift of the suffering Servant (Isaiah 53).

Further, the goodness or kindness of God leads to repentance (Romans 2:4). His patient and providential working in history is to encourage men to seek Him (Acts 17:24–27).

Finally, God shows His goodness in His special care for His people. He rules and overrules every event on earth for the ultimate good of His people (Romans 8:28–29).

Rejecting or Doubting His Goodness

In spite of God being good, many people reject or doubt this goodness. They doubt God despite His many demonstrations of goodness mentioned earlier. Yet the Scriptures warn that when people despise God's kindness and patience, they store up God's wrath for themselves, which He will display at the final judgment.

Or do you think lightly of the riches of His kindness and tolerance and patience, not knowing that the kindness of God leads you to repentance? But because of your

stubbornness and unrepentant heart you are storing up
wrath for yourself in the day of wrath and revelation of
the righteous judgment of God. (Romans 2:4–5)

God gets no pleasure in the death of the wicked but rather
rejoices in their repentance (Ezekiel 33:11). He yearns for
man to escape His judgment. He is slow to wrath, warns
before He judges, and also provides a way to escape His
judgment. And, as mentioned earlier, out of His goodness
God gives the gift of His Son. God sent His Son into the
world not to judge it but that we could be delivered from His
judgment (John 3:17).

The underlying motivation of all sin is a doubt in God's
goodness. In other words we would never sin unless we
thought something good would come out of it. The Serpent
deceived Eve in this way and uses his deceitful lies against
men and women every day (see Genesis 3:1–6).

If sin withholds good from us, why would we sin (see
Jeremiah 5:25)? It is because we are deceived. For this reason
we need daily exhortation not to be hardened in this deceit
(Hebrews 3:13).

Some look at the evil, pain, and suffering in the world and
then look at God and blame Him and doubt His goodness.
We need to first look at God and marvel at how man could
rebel against His goodness and mess up the paradise that
He created.

Others fixate upon a certain expectation or dream that
they desire. In their minds is this thought: *God, if You are
truly good, this is what You should do.*

A friend's mother was very sick, and we prayed for her.
When she was not healed, the man became cold and disin-
terested in the Lord.

An intelligent and gifted young man told me once why he was not interested in the Lord. He said that when he was a small boy he loved football. His physical size hindered his ability to excel, but he would pray that God would help him. He said, "It didn't work. I decided I could not trust God." This is different than my father-in-law, who at his eightieth birthday party, said he had never been disappointed. He had suffered numerous setbacks and had been cheated of millions of dollars. However, he had also learned to rest in God's good will, which he knew was what was truly best when evaluated from eternity's perspective.

Do you doubt God's goodness to you? We all will be tempted to do so. I used to look at God through the glasses of my guilty conscience. With this viewpoint I sensed that God was very reluctant to bless me. One week God gave me a new pair of glasses. I began to look at God through the glasses of Christ. I began to view the God whom Jesus revealed — the One who "is *kind* to ungrateful and evil men" (Luke 6:35, italics added). My life began to be transformed and my heart began to be won over to my good God whom I now perceived as One who yearned to bless me. Why not ask God to give you this new pair of glasses as well?

Complaining about His Goodness

Temptation is a common experience to all of God's people (1 Corinthians 10:13), and one common temptation is to grumble and complain (1 Corinthians 10:10–11). None of us is above it. When we grumble and complain, we disobey the kind command of Philippians 2:14–15 and invite God's loving discipline (cf. Numbers 11:1) as well as lose our witness to the world. Thus Paul encourages us to "do all things without grumbling or disputing; so that you will prove yourselves to be blameless and innocent, children of God above reproach in the midst of a crooked and perverse generation, among whom you appear as lights in the world" (Philippians 2:14–15).

The answer is not to curb only our outward grumbling and stuff it inside of ourselves. The answer is to seek God and work out the matter with Him.

When we complain, we have lost sight of God's past goodness, are not discerning His present goodness, and are not anticipating His future goodness. As we have stated, we need to recall that we have earned God's judgment. Anything I ever received in life other than His judgment is due to the grace of God! We need to also discern that God is sovereign and can overrule the most horrible events to bring about our ultimate good (Genesis 50:20; Romans 8:28–29).

Knowing Him

His Goodness Past, Present, and Future

When we complain, we have lost sight of God's past goodness, are not discerning His present goodness, and are not anticipating His future goodness. Remember, we have earned God's judgment. Anything we ever receive in life other than His judgment is due to the grace of God! We need not grumble or complain if we know God always has the ultimate good for us, both in His plans and actions.

When We Grow Weary
in Doing Good Things

Our good God desires us to do good to all men (Galatians 6:10). However, we will all be tempted to "lose heart in doing good" (Galatians 6:9). People will be tempted to think that "it is vain to serve God" (Malachi 3:14). Our wonderful Savior has been tempted in all ways and promises to come to our aid when we are tempted (Hebrews 2:18).

Note how Isaiah prophesied of this temptation that the Messiah would experience:

He said to Me, "You are My Servant, Israel, in Whom I will show My glory."
But I said, "I have toiled in vain, I have spent My strength for nothing and vanity." (Isaiah 49:3–4a)

How did the Lord answer this temptation? Despite feeling He had labored in vain, the Messiah rested in two truths: "Yet surely the justice due to Me is with the Lord, and My reward with My God" (Isaiah 49:4b).

It is always worth it to serve the Lord. Our toil is never in vain (1 Corinthians 15:58). It is only a matter of time and the reward will come (Galatians 6:9). Even first-century slaves received this promise. "With good will render service, as to the Lord, and not to men, knowing that whatever good thing each one does, this he will receive back from the Lord, whether slave or free" (Ephesians 6:7–8).

The Christian life is a battle, but it is a "good fight." We are to confess our Lord, but it is a "good confession." The words that the Spirit will inspire us to speak are "good" words (Ephesians 4:29). The works that He has preordained that we walk in are "good" works that are to spring from a "good" conscience (1 Timothy 1:5). Our God is good—all the time. We are in a battle, but depend on Him to renew your spirit and keep you going.

Carrying Our Burdens
Rather than Relying on His Goodness

Sometimes we leave His goodness because of burdens we choose to bear without His help. Our good God desires to help us. The command to cast our cares on the Lord is based on a truth that He cares for us (1 Peter 5:7). When you doubt His goodness and care for you, you tend to bear your burdens on your own shoulders. In fact, the more something means to you, the greater the urge to try to control the situation.

The folly is that we trust our own self-interest and ability more than our good and omnipotent God. He alone is able to take care of what we commit to Him (2 Timothy 1:12). He alone can give us the promise to never ultimately disappoint us (Romans 10:11).

When Abraham offered up Isaac on the altar (Genesis 22), James tells us that his faith was perfected (James 2:22). The idea of "perfected" is being brought to a divinely appointed goal. God's goal for Abraham—as it is for us—was to be trained to trust Him with the most precious thing in his life. Will you trust God with your Isaac? Will you place it in His hands at this moment? Will you put your finger on 1 Peter 5:7 and tell God that you want to fully obey it?

Doubting His Goodness
Because We Doubt His Word

God's commandments are for our good (see Deuteronomy 10:13). His commandments are not burdensome (1 John 5:3). When He tells us to do something, He is pointing out the best path of life for us. When He forbids us from doing something, He is seeking to protect us from harm and that which would not be best for us. God desires that you have an implicit trust in His goodness that is behind His kind words. He is waiting for you to discover this for yourself and "taste and see that the Lord is good" (Psalm 34:8). A heart that digests, remembers, and acts on God's words so as to bear fruit is called a "good heart" (Luke 8:15).

Doubting His Goodness Due to
Our Failure to Understand James 1:17

As God looks at mankind, He sees no one who does good (Romans 3:12). In His goodness, He offers the good gift of His Son, and with this gift comes everything we will ever need (Romans 8:32). If you understand this, you can agree with the psalmists, who say, "I have no good besides You" (Psalm 16:2), and, "The nearness of God is my good" (Psalm 73:28). A failure to agree with these statements is to be blind to the truth that "every good thing given and every perfect gift" comes from God (James 1:17).

I have made it a practice to review every day and briefly journal some of the good gifts that come from God's good hand. Once a week I look back on the week's blessing and on the blessing of this same week in past years. I recommend you do the same. When we are able to recognize God's gifts, we are able to rejoice in the good that God has given us (Deuteronomy 26:11). Do this and you will thank (Psalm 106:1) and praise (Psalm 147:12) your good God. And surely the Giver of every good and perfect gift is worthy of our gratitude and praise.

Note

1. For more insight into expressing honest, true repentance before God, see Bill Thrasher, *A Journey to Victorious Praying* (Chicago: Moody, 2003), 29–32.

Part Six

A GLORIOUS GOD

19

The Glorious
Name of God

DISCOVERING
THE REASON FOR LIVING

GOD'S GLORY REFERS to His divine nature and the revelation of His attributes. In a similar vein, His name also is associated with His divine person. Therefore to live for His name is to live for God—to glorify God is to simply affirm the perfections of His revealed character.

God's glory and His name are described as great (Psalm 138:5). His name is also described as awesome (Deuteronomy 28:58), majestic (Psalm 8:1), holy (Psalm 33:21), good (Psalm 52:9), everlasting (Psalm 135:13), and strong (Proverbs 18:10).

In other words, His attributes are descriptions of His name and His glory. For this reason the Scriptures speak of "the glory of His grace" (Ephesians 1:6) and "the glory of His power" (2 Thessalonians 1:9).

The infinite value and resources of His character led Paul

to write of the "riches of His glory" (Ephesians 3:16; see Philippians 4:19). God will not give His glory to another (Isaiah 48:11). He is unique and to be exalted (Psalm 148:13) and honored above all (Deuteronomy 28:58). The climax of the revelation of God is in Jesus (Hebrews 1:2–3), whose name is above every name (Philippians 2:9). One day all will acknowledge our glorious God (Philippians 2:10–11), and even today we have the opportunity to bow our knee to Him and to acknowledge Him for who He is!

How God Displays His Glorious Name

God displays His glorious name through all His actions, which flow out of His glorious character. His creation (Psalm 19:1), His work in redeeming Israel (Exodus 9:16; 2 Samuel 7:23; Daniel 9:15), His caring for the helpless (Isaiah 25:3–4), His sending Christ into the world (Luke 2:20), His working miracles through Christ (Mark 2:12; John 2:11; 11:4), His raising Christ from the dead (Romans 6:4), His granting salvation to people (Acts 11:18; Romans 15:9) — all these works display His glory. So do the judging of His enemies (Isaiah 24:16, 24), the fulfilling of His promises (Isaiah 60:21; 61:3), and the glorifying of His Son (John 8:54; 17:5).

God is concerned (Ezekiel 20:9, 14, 22, 44) and jealous (Ezekiel 39:25) for His holy name and will both act for the sake of His name and vindicate the holiness of His name (Ezekiel 36:25). This truth is a great comfort when you see the goodness of His name! He makes a name for Himself and glorifies Himself not at His people's expense but for their benefit. God's glory is not like a man who seeks to use and misuse people solely to benefit himself. God glorifies Himself by sharing His resources with us (Philippians 4:19; 2 Peter 1:3). He makes His glory known to us by showing us mercy (Romans 9:23), offering us acceptance (Romans 15:7), guiding His people (Psalms 23:3; 31:3), and forgiving us (Psalms 25:11; 79:9; 1 John 2:12). His glory is shown also in His answering our prayers (John 14:13) and leading His people into rest (Isaiah 63:14). He even shows His glory by glorifying His people (Romans 8:17, 30; John 17:22).

Spurning the Glorious Name of God

The Bible says all of us have sinned and fallen short of the righteous standards that His glory demands (Romans 3:23). For this reason God sent His Son who is called the Lord of glory. What happened? Man spurned the Lord of glory. The greatest crime ever committed on Planet Earth was the crucifixion of this Lord of glory (1 Corinthians 2:8)!

God continues to seek to reveal Himself to all people, but the sad commentary is the rejection of the light of revelation and the exchanging of the glory of the incorruptible God for temporal idols (see Romans 1:23). Such idolatry is a refusal to glorify the God who controls our very next life breath (see Daniel 5:23). Such a response involves glorying in that for which we should be ashamed (Philippians 3:19). God is kind and patient to offer repentance, but many will still choose not to repent and give Him glory even in the final chapter of human history (Revelation 16:9). Those who do not accept their dignified role as a creature in God's image but who seek to exalt themselves in place of their Creator will be judged (see Acts 12:23).

The aim of the Devil — whose name means "slanderer" —

is to promote the blasphemy or slander of God's name through the hypocrisy and sin of God's people (Romans 2:24; Isaiah 52:5). Yet many accept the Devil's lies. Those who do are "a foolish people" for spurning God's name, the psalmist says (Psalm 74:18).

True believers who follow Christ are identified by His glorious name (Matthew 18:20; 28:19). Satan hates the name of God and inspires a hatred for those who are identified with it (Matthew 10:22; 24:9; Luke 21:12; John 15:21). The persecutors who exclude and abuse God's people will one day be put to shame (Isaiah 66:5), but those who are reviled will be blessed, for the Spirit of glory will rest on them (1 Peter 4:14)!

A Description of Worship

To be obsessed with the glorious name of God puts us in perfect balance, because we are in touch with reality (see how worship affected Nebuchadnezzar's mental health in Daniel 4:34). Praise is the logical response to the revelation of God's name or character (Psalm 48:10). To glorify Him is to praise Him and stand in awe of His revealed attributes (Psalm 22:23). It is to simply ascribe to Him the glory that is due His name (Psalm 29:2). Because His name is glorious (1 Chronicles 29:13), His praise is to be glorious (Psalm 66:2).

We worship God when in our thoughts, affections, and emotions, we acknowledge His character. The psalmist appeals to himself to bless or praise God with "all that is within me" (Psalm 103:1) and to unite his heart to fear God's name (Psalm 86:11). The apostle glorifies God for His sovereign plan (Romans 11:36), wisdom (Romans 16:27), His rule (1 Timothy 1:17), and His salvation (2 Timothy 4:18). The heavenly scenes of worship glorify Him as the sovereign Creator (Revelation 4:9, 11), for His attributes (Revelation 7:12), and for His judgment (Revelation 11:13).

The very mention of Christ to the enlightened mind evokes a response of worship on earth (Galatians 1:5; Hebrews 13:21), in heaven (Revelation 5:12), and forever (2 Peter 3:18). His is the only name in which one can find salvation (Acts 4:12).[1]

The thing that will be so glorious about heaven is that all who are there will glorify their wonderful God forever. With a loud voice they will declare, "Worthy is the Lamb that was slain to receive power and riches and wisdom and might and honor and glory and blessing" (Revelation 5:12).

As we await that future time of ongoing, joyous worship, we can worship Him today, right now. Our good God places many benefits into the lives of genuine worshipers. In my book *A Journey to Victorious Praying,* I have an entire chapter entitled "Experiencing the Goodness of Praise," which explores eight benefits that happen as a by-product of worship.[2]

Yet many continue in their refusal to glorify God. This has led to the devolution of man (Romans 1:21). One day, however, all will glorify Him (Revelation 15:4; Philippians 2:9–11) and even in some way His inanimate creation (Isaiah 43:20). We have the awesome privilege of doing it now.

Our worship should flow naturally in response to the reality of God's great name. Look at the following twenty-eight biblical responses to the revelation of God's glorious name:

- We can serve in His name (Deuteronomy 18:5).
- We can speak in His name (Deuteronomy 18:22).

- We can bless in His name (Deuteronomy 21:5; 2 Samuel 6:18).
- We can come in His name (1 Samuel 17:45).
- We can magnify His name (2 Samuel 7:26).
- We can praise His name (2 Samuel 22:50).
- We can confess His name (1 Kings 8:33).
- We can call on His name (1 Kings 18:24).
- We can glory in His holy name (1 Chronicles 16:10).
- We can love His name (Psalm 5:11).
- We can know His name (Psalm 9:10).
- We can boast in His name (Psalm 20:7).
- We can tell of His name (Psalm 22:22).
- We can ascribe to the Lord the glory due His name (Psalm 29:2).
- We can trust His name (Psalm 33:21; John 1:12).
- We can exalt His name (Psalm 34:3).
- We can unite our heart to fear His name (Psalm 86:11).
- We can cause His name to be remembered (Psalm 45:17).
- We can lift up our hands in His name (Psalm 63:4).
- We can sing the glory of His name (Psalm 66:2).
- We can seek His name (Psalm 83:16).
- We can rejoice in His name (Psalm 89:16).
- We can remember His name (Psalm 119:55).
- We can wait on His name (Isaiah 26:8).
- We can take refuge in His name (Zephaniah 3:12).
- We can esteem His name (Malachi 3:16).
- We can hope in His name (Matthew 12:21).
- We can pray in His name (John 14:13–14).

Our Future Hope of Glory

Worship will continue one day on a new earth, where the glorious name of the King will be exalted. Christ's future kingdom will be glorious because it will be a glorious display of the Messiah (Isaiah 4:2). The very earth will be filled with the knowledge of the glory of the Lord (Habakkuk 2:14). This will follow the glorious appearing (Titus 2:13) of our Lord, who will rapture His church and also come later with all His glory and establish His kingdom (Matthew 16:27; 24:30; 25:31).

As we behold our Lord's character, we can be changed from one degree of glory to the other (2 Corinthians 3:18). Our hope is to one day be revealed with Him in glory (Colossians 1:27; 3:4). God has prepared us for glory (Romans 9:23) and called us to experience eternal glory (2 Timothy 2:10; 1 Peter 5:10). This will involve all our future blessings, which include even a new glorious body (Philippians 3:21).

We will glorify God when we experience our future hope in heaven (Revelation 19:7). The new earth will need neither sun or moon, for it will be illuminated by the glory of God (Revelation 21:23). This future hope is what enables us to put any present suffering in perspective. That's why the apostle Paul could write, "I consider that the sufferings of this present time are not worthy to be compared with the glory that is to be revealed to us" (Romans 8:18).

A Purpose for Living

God motivated by His goodness desires to glorify Himself. If you were perfect in every way — your motivations, words, and actions — the greatest gift you could give somebody would be to allow the person to enjoy you for who you are. All of God's actions (Ephesians 1:11) are for the praise of His glory (Ephesians 1:12, 14).

In fearful rebellion to God, man and woman each seek to make a name for themselves (see Genesis 11:4). Christ's liberating death has freed us to discover a purpose bigger than living for ourselves.

> For the love of Christ controls us, having concluded this, that one died for all, therefore all died; and He died for all, so that they who live might no longer live for themselves, but for Him who died and rose again on their behalf. (2 Corinthians 5:14–15)

In the enablement of the Spirit, we can say with the psalmist, "Not to us, O Lord, not to us, but to Your name give glory because of Your lovingkindness, because of Your truth" (Psalm 115:1).

If you speak to one whose heart is broken and discouraged and you draw attention to yourself, what have you accomplished? They may be impressed with you but still find no comfort or hope. If the Lord's character is exalted, there is hope, comfort, and encouragement for everyone.

There is authority, hope, and salvation in God's glorious name. At His name, one day every knee will bow and glorify Him (Philippians 2:9–11). We are under His holy command to in no way take His name in vain but to rather sanctify and hallow it (Matthew 6:9). The ultimate motivation of one's service is His name's sake (Romans 1:5).

When we are in need, we utter our petitions to our merciful God to meet us at our point of need. However, we are mature beyond that. Our ultimate motivation is to display to the world our glorious Shepherd (Psalms 23:3; 31:3). We cry to God for cleansing from sin but also humbly receive God's provision to allow God to display His gracious name in forgiving us. As the psalmist cried out, so should we: "Help us, O God of our salvation, for the glory of Your name; and deliver us and forgive our sins for Your name's sake" (Psalm 79:9).

All of life—even the mundane—is an opportunity to live to display God's glorious character. "Whether, then, you eat or drink or whatever you do, do all to the glory of God" (1 Corinthians 10:31).

Knowing Him

Acting in His Name

When an athlete's name is placed upon a piece of sporting equipment, it symbolizes his endorsement of that piece of equipment. Similarly, all of our actions are to be done in the name of God, that is, to have His endorsement on all of our words and actions (Colossians 3:17).

Our concern is to not do anything that would give an opportunity for others to speak evil against His glorious name (1 Timothy 6:1). Instead, all of life—even the mundane—is an opportunity for us to live to display God's glorious character. "Whether, then, you eat or drink or whatever you do, do all to the glory of God" (1 Corinthians 10:31)

Practical Ways to Glorify God

What are specific practical ways the Scripture gives us to glorify God?

- Confess your sins and tell the truth (Joshua 7:19).
- Take time to thank Him for His blessings (Luke 17:15, 18).
- Believe Him to fulfill His promises (Romans 4:20; 2 Corinthians 1:20).
- Obey God's promptings to give to others (2 Corinthians 8:19; 9:13; cf. Haggai 1:8).
- Discover and use your spiritual gifts to help others (1 Peter 4:11).
- Do the good works that God enables you to do (Matthew 5:16).
- Suffer for righteousness (1 Peter 2:12; 4:16).
- Keep your body pure for God's purposes (1 Corinthians 6:20).
- Abide in the Lord and bear much fruit (John 15:8).
- Honor God in whatever way He wills for you to die (John 21:19).

We find God's people appealing to His name to mercifully act on their behalf (Psalm 109:21; Jeremiah 14:7, 21). When you find others who are also living for the sake of God's glorious name, know that they are worthy of your support as well (3 John 7–8).

Why not right now ask God to revive your life to live for His glory so that He would be glorified through you to the greatest possible extent (Psalm 143:11). You will never regret any sacrifice that you will ever make to live for His name.

Jesus Himself said when we value His name above our homes and even our family, we "will receive many times as much" (Matthew 19:29).

The early church considered it a great honor to be worthy to suffer for Christ's name (Acts 5:41). Note that as God worked changes in Paul's life and people heard about this work, they glorified God:

> I was still unknown by sight to the churches of Judea which were in Christ; but only, they kept hearing, "He who once persecuted us is now preaching the faith which he once tried to destroy." And they were glorifying God because of me. (Galatians 1:22–24)

Will you put your finger on Galatians 1:24 and give your life to the Lord and tell Him to be glorified to the fullest possible extent through your life? There is no greater cause to live for! May God abundantly answer your prayer. I will pray with you, and please pray for me in the same way.

Notes

1. For further description of the meaning of true worship, see Bill Thrasher, *A Journey to Victorious Praying* (Chicago: Moody, 2003), 207–12.
2. Ibid., 199–206. For practical steps in developing a lifetime of worship, see pages 219–23 in *A Journey to Victorious Praying*.

**To download the free study guide
please visit www.victoriouspraying.com**